Viet Cong and NVA Tunnels and Fortifications of the Vietnam War

G Rottman • Illustrated by C Taylor, A Mallinson & L Ray

Series editors Marcus Cowper and Nikolai Bogdanovic

First published in 2006 by Osprey Publishing
Midland House, West Way, Botley, Oxford OX2 0PH, UK
443 Park Avenue South, New York, NY 10016, USA
E-mail: info@ospreypublishing.com

ISBN-13: 978 1 84603 003 1

Cartography: Map Studio, Romsey, UK
Typeset in Monotype Gill Sans and ITC Stone Serif
Design: Ken Vail Graphic Design, Cambridge, UK
Index by Alison Worthington
Originated by United Graphics, Singapore
Printed and bound in China through Bookbuilders

07 08 09 10 11   11 10 9 8 7 6 5 4 3 2

A CIP catalog record for this book is available from the British Library.

FOR A CATALOGUE OF ALL BOOKS PUBLISHED BY OSPREY MILITARY AND AVIATION
PLEASE CONTACT:

Osprey Direct, c/o Random House Distribution Center, 400 Hahn Road,
Westminster, MD 21157
Email: info@ospreydirect.com

Osprey Direct UK, P.O. Box 140, Wellingborough, Northants, NN8 2FA, UK
E-mail: info@ospreydirect.co.uk

www.ospreypublishing.com

Acknowledgments

The author is indebted to Laurent Touchard for his research
assistance, Steve Sherman of RADIX Press for the use of
materials, and Bruce Hanesalo of Military/Info Publishing for
the use of illustrations from *Tunnel Warfare*, Vol. 4: *Asian Tunnel
Warfare*. All photographs and illustrations are US Army unless
otherwise credited.

Measurements

To covert figures given in the US system of inches and feet
to metric, and vice versa, the following conversion formulas
are provided:

1 inch	2.54cm
1 foot	0.3048m
1 yard	0.9144m
1 mile	1.609km
1 pound	0.4536kg
1 ounce	28.35 grams

1 millimetre (mm)	0.0394 in.
1 centimetre (cm)	0.3937 in.
1 metre (m)	1.0936 yards
1 kilometre (km)	0.6214 miles
1 gram (g)	0.035 ounces
1 kilogram (kg)	2.2046 lb

The Fortress Study Group (FSG)

The object of the FSG is to advance the education of the public
in the study of all aspects of fortifications and their armaments,
especially works constructed to mount or resist artillery.
The FSG holds an annual conference in September over a long
weekend with visits and evening lectures, an annual tour abroad
lasting about eight days, and an annual Members' Day.
The FSG journal *FORT* is published annually, and its newsletter
Casemate is published three times a year. Membership is
international. For further details, please contact:

The Secretary, c/o 6 Lanark Place, London W9 1BS, UK

Contents

Introduction

The elaborate fortifications that our Marines were forced to attack – the hundreds of meters of neck-deep bunkers, fighting holes, gun pits, and connecting trenches so cleverly woven into the hedgerows, buildings, and thickets – were constructed over the previous weeks by the full-time efforts of a local VC support battalion. [A US Marine Corps officer]

The fortifications were unbelievable, and the NVA soldiers were popping in and out, up and down, shooting from all the holes. Fields of fire overlapped. To get at one bunker, you had to take the fire from another. By teams and pairs the Marines would throw grenades, then flank the bunker, and fire up the trench. It was not our first time out. As usual, the enemy was almost invisible until we got right on top of them. Some broke and ran – most died in place. [A US Marine Corps officer]

ARVN soldiers rush past a typical Vietnamese rural house, commonly called a "hootch" by US troops. The walls are made from thatch and the roof is of red clay tiles. (Nyuyên Ngoc Hanh)

In Vietnamese villages the women did much of the work; here they are hauling 50kg rice sacks, which were reused as sandbags. The thatched hootch is built on stilts and the underside is closed off with barbed wire to corral pigs and goats.

The war in Vietnam was characterized by evolving tactics and techniques, and seemingly conflicting means of warfare, all set within a complex political environment. It is often described as a guerrilla war, though it was also a conventional one for the United States involving multiple-division operations. The Viet Cong (VC) Main Forces and the People's Army of Vietnam (PAVN) or North Vietnamese Army (NVA) regulars may not have been supported by artillery, tanks, and aircraft (except in rare instances), but nonetheless they conducted large-scale conventional operations against the Free World military forces.

In taking on the Free World forces, the VC/NVA faced tremendous firepower delivered by artillery, mortars, direct-fire weapons, fighter-bombers, strategic bombers, and helicopter gunships. The weight of ordnance dumped on the elusive fighters met and often superseded that delivered in World War II on major population centers and Pacific islands.

Free World forces also possessed effective surveillance, reconnaissance, and human intelligence collection capabilities. However, the vast area of operations, dense tropical vegetation, and rugged terrain to some degree countered these capabilities. The VC/NVA needed other means to reduce the huge disparity between the belligerents. They became highly adept at camouflage and counter-intelligence measures (or "asymmetric innovation" in today's terminology). Their tactics also reflected attempts to counter the massive firepower they faced. They moved at night, often rapidly covering great distances to limit their exposure; they widely dispersed deploying units; and when directly engaging the enemy they employed "belt-hugging" tactics (moving in and remaining closely engaged), even intermingling units, to prevent the enemy from bringing his artillery and close air support to bear.

This Vietnamese hootch in the Mekong Delta is made entirely of palm thatch on the roof and walls. Part of the front wall is made of bamboo latticework. Note the nipa palms growing around the hootch, a primary source of thatching.

It became critically important for the VC/NVA to conceal and protect themselves from prying eyes and massive firepower. Soldiers have always dug, but the VC/NVA combatants dug as few soldiers ever have done before, with the exceptions of those during World War I and the Korean War, both to hide and to survive. Their field works included defended villages, base camps, fortified complexes, hilltop defenses, trench systems, individual fighting positions, crew-served weapons positions, bunkers, caches, and extensive tunnel systems. Camouflage measures to hide from ground and aerial observation, deception measures, and the employment of obstacles and booby traps went hand-in-hand with such works. The maintenance of their trail systems was also of critical importance.

Field fortifications and tunnel systems are typically thought of as defensive in nature and as active protective measures, but the VC/NVA also employed them offensively. It was common for extensive field works, weapons positions, and shelters to be constructed to support assaults and sieges on Free World firebases and remote camps, and even for large-scale ambushes.

Free World Civilian Irregular Defense Group strikers undergoing training in a rubber plantation. Rubber plantations were devoid of underbrush and provided good protection from aerial observation. However, these trees are immature and lack the dense tops. The plantation floors were covered with dead leaves. (Author's collection)

The tunnel systems were begun in the late 1940s and evolved through the First Indochina War with France. They were first used to hide wanted individuals, then families as the fighting worsened, and to hide supplies; before long whole villages and guerrilla units were hiding in them. They were well developed by the time the Americans arrived in 1965 and continued to expand as Free World firepower increased.

The nature of the land and the war

Climate and terrain

The vegetation, climate and geography of Vietnam had major effects on the tactics and techniques of the belligerent parties, which in turn influenced the character of fortifications, leading the VC/NVA to use different designs and materials in different areas. The Republic of Vietnam (RVN – South Vietnam) consisted of some 66,200 square miles (slightly smaller than Washington state) of widely diverse terrain. The country was some 700 miles in length north to south and between 30 and 150 miles in width.

A narrow 10–30-mile-wide plain bordered about three-quarters of the length of the RVN's South China Sea coast. The terrain was level or gently rolling, with broad valleys of slow-moving rivers and marshes. The vegetation comprised vast areas of rice paddies, and areas consisting of woodland, brush, and bamboo. Much of the country's population lived on the plain, and as a result the agricultural and commercial centers were also located there. Well-developed highway, road, and railroad systems served the region. As a result much action took place on the coastal plains and significant Free World forces were deployed there to protect the population and resources.

A scout dog and his handler cross a VC-built footbridge, typical of the crude but effective VC construction techniques. Scout and tracker dogs were useful for locating tunnel entrances and air vents as well as hidden bunkers and supply caches.

The central highlands covered much of the inland northern and central portions of the country from the 17th Parallel Demilitarized Zone (DMZ). In the north the forested mountains rose up to 5,000ft., gradually decreasing in elevation and ruggedness as they ran south. The mountains, hills, and ridges were intermingled with valleys, plateaux, and deep river gorges. The forests, usually double-canopy, often had only light underbrush. There were also areas of brush, elephant grass, and bamboo. The road system was poorly developed, and cross-country movement was difficult. The area was sparsely populated, mostly by primitive Montagnard tribesmen. The VC/NVA established large base areas – main bases (*Han Cu*) – in the remote mountain valleys, as they could only be easily reached by helicopter from the Free World bases along the coast. The VC/NVA could easily access these border areas from Laos and then use them as advance bases for operating in the RVN.

In the west-central part of the country on the Laotian border lay a highland plateau, covering a 40 by 100-mile area. This was mostly covered with brush and high grasses. The funnel-shaped piedmont region defined the south end of the central highlands. It was covered by a rolling terrain of double- and triple-canopy forests and underbrush with scattered patches of bamboo or elephant grass, as well as rubber plantations. In the southeast portion toward the coast lay extensive cultivated areas and a larger population; the road network was widespread, but remote areas were still

present. A great deal of action took place in this region due to VC efforts to control the large population, and major base areas ("war zones") were established further inland near the Cambodian border, across which they found sanctuary.

The southern quarter of the country was covered by a lowland plain, the Mekong Delta. Saigon sat at the juncture of the piedmont, the southern end of the coastal plain, and the Delta. The Delta was characterized by vast rice paddies and marshes with some wooded areas and swampland. The Delta was coursed by rivers, streams, and canals, the primary means of transportation. With the exception of the Delta and scattered swamps and marshes, most areas were well drained.

Red and yellow podzolic soils (heavily leached in the upper layers with a accumulation of granular materials in the lower ones) characterized half of the land area, with reddish-brown laterite soils covering about 10 percent of the total. These soil types dominated the central highlands. Alluvial soils were to be found in the Mekong Delta, as were peat and muck soils. Gray podzolic soils were to be found in parts of the highlands together with black loam and laterite. Soft brown soils, clay, and sand were found along the coast.

Most of the trees were hardwood evergreens, which provided excellent concealment from ground and air observation all year round. Ground vegetation, brush, vines, and grasses also provided excellent concealment, even at close range. Although often described as jungles, the forests were not true jungles or rainforests. Rubber plantations were planted in neat rows girded by straight roads, and were mostly devoid of underbrush. Cultivated areas were found throughout the country, growing vegetables, sugarcane, fruit, and rice.

The village (*Xa* or *Làng*) lay at the heart of Vietnamese peasant society, and could be populated by anything from a hundred people up to several thousand. A village complex might consist of two or more small hamlets (*Âp*) within a few hundred meters of each other or up to a dozen spread over many kilometers. There were also isolated hamlets.

Vietnam experiences two seasons. The southwest monsoon, or wet season, sees warm humid air flowing inland from the sea from mid-May to early October. The humid airflow brings heavy tropical rains to the western slopes of the mountains, with an average rainfall of 55–110in. in the north and 40–95in.

in the south. The eastern slopes and coastal plains receive comparatively little rain. High humidity and temperatures prevail. The northeast monsoon, or dry season, occurs when Asia's interior high pressure forces dry, cool air toward the sea between early November and mid-March. The coastal plains receive heavy rain. From January into March the coastal and mountain areas experience the *crachin*, a period of intermittent drizzle and low overcast clouds. From mid-March to mid-May very high temperatures and humidity are experienced and days are often cloudy and overcast. Early October to early November sees heavy rain and cloud along the coast.

While the road network was unevenly developed and there were many mountainous, marsh, and swamp areas, 46 percent of the country could be traversed by armored vehicles (tanks and armored personnel carriers) year-round. Armor could maneuver in much of the coastal plain and piedmont. In the dry season even larger areas were accessible by armor, even some areas in the Delta. However, armor was generally restricted to roads and trails in the Delta and the highlands.

The opposing forces

The NVA consisted of regular troops, and VC Main Force units were mostly filled with North Vietnamese, even before the 1968 Tet Offensive decimated the VC. It is a mistake to call NVA and VC Main Force guerrillas

A bomb-blasted NVA communication trench connecting fighting/living bunkers outside of Khe Sanh. This one has a low parapet camouflaged with reeds and elephant grass. (US Marine Corps)

merely because they employed unconventional tactics. Local VC guerrillas supported them and this was still an aspect of the war, but for the most part from 1965 (when US combat units were introduced) Vietnam was a low-intensity conventional conflict; American solders were fighting light, conventional forces that had adapted their tactics to the terrain and in order to match the firepower and mobility of Free World forces. Local Force VC and their supporters conducted harassment and sabotage raids, collected intelligence, disseminated propaganda, collected "war taxes" from locals, pressed locals into forced labor, served as guides, and provided other support to transiting NVA and Main Force units.

There were three critical factors that benefited the North Vietnamese. (1) The United States restricted itself with self-imposed constraints, both militarily and diplomatically, mainly because of the very real fear of provoking intervention by China and the USSR. (2) The North Vietnamese made maximum use of sanctuaries in Laos and Cambodia for their supply and staging bases. (3) Extensive material and training support were provided by China and the USSR. The NVA conducted a "protracted war" to wear down the political and military will and the morale of the United States. They avoided set-piece battles unless success looked likely, and undertook measures to protect their forces from massive Free World firepower. The wide and innovative use of tunnels and fortifications contributed to this goal.

A fresh 750 lb. bomb crater in laterite soil. In the background are elephant grass and bamboo. Such craters were of little use to the VC/NVA, as camouflaging vegetation was blown away from the immediate area. (Author's collection)

The author delivers a WP grenade into a Montagnard hootch in an abandoned village occupied by the VC. The hootch is made of nipa palm thatching, corrugated sheet metal, and bamboo. In the foreground are sandbag bomb shelters braced with barbed-wire picket stakes, built by the former inhabitants. The curved aluminum sheet between the two semi-sunken shelters was taken from an Air Force "speed pallet" for use as roofing. (Author's collection)

Building and manning the defenses

VC/NVA fortifications, tunnels, and bases for the most part were constructed by the users. Units built their own facilities, but there were some external sources of assistance. Local civilians were often impressed through coercion, mutual agreement, or voluntarily, depending on loyalties. The loyalty of the civilians employed would naturally dictate the facilities on which they were allowed to work. It was not uncommon for civilians to notify Free World forces of the presence and location of tunnels and base camps. They would also guide them to the site and might be familiar with its layout, having been forced to build it. Often VC Local Force units would prepare positions and camps for transiting NVA and Main Force units. Local Force and Self-Defense units would also maintain existing unoccupied camps and facilities in addition to looking after trails and caches.

VC/NVA units

VC/NVA units were so widely diverse in organization, strength, and armament that only generalities can be presented here. Just as they adapted their fortifications and field works to local conditions and the mission, so they did with unit organization and equipment.

VC/NVA divisions usually possessed an engineer battalion (*Cong Binh Tieu Doan*). They were often employed to build and improve roads and trails, especially inside Cambodia and Laos. They built divisional command posts, dumps, and caches for munitions and supplies, and were involved in the camouflage of these facilities. Engineers provided little support to the division's combat units and when not employed in construction tasks were used as transport troops. The small regimental engineer companies provided some support, but were limited to hand tools. A large number of engineer, bridge building, and river crossing regiments and independent battalions were organized, but these mainly worked inside Laos and Cambodia operating and maintaining the trail network and logistics system; they comprised 97,000 full-time troops and up to 500,000 part-time impressed civilians. Sapper units, often compared to US assault engineers, acted

A US Marine checks out a hamlet bomb shelter constructed of two bamboo walls with approximately a foot of earth fill between them. The roof is made of hardwood logs. (US Marine Corps)

11

The two entrances into a VC bunker after the camouflage has been removed. The overhead cover is provided by a combination of hardwood logs and banana palm. The pan was used to remove spoil. The ground is covered by tan-colored bamboo leaves and husks, an excellent camouflaging material. (Leroy "Red" Wilson)

as reconnaissance commandos and were not directly involved in construction, other than that of their own positions and camps. Besides their usual infiltration missions they reconnoitered routes and sites for bases and positions as well as installing booby traps.

A full-strength NVA infantry division (*Su Doan Bo Binh*) had 9,600 troops organized into three infantry regiments; an artillery regiment or battalion in some instances; antiaircraft, engineer, signal, and medical battalions; and a transport company. The artillery regiments were mostly armed with 82mm and 120mm mortars.

Infantry regiments were about 2,500 strong, with three 600-man battalions. Most units were frequently understrength with battalions typically numbering 300–500 soldiers. Regardless of organization tables, the armament of the NVA units varied considerably because of long campaigning, weapons availability, and how they were configured for specific operations. Regiments typically had a recoilless rifle company with 8–12 Soviet 73mm SPG-9 or 85mm B-10 recoilless guns, or Chinese 75mm Type 52 and 57mm Type 36 recoilless rifles (collectively called DKZs – *Dai-bac Khong Ziat*); a mortar company with six to eight 82mm PM37 or 120mm PM43 mortars; an antiaircraft company with six to ten 12.7mm DShKM38/46 machine guns; plus small engineer, transport, signal, and medical companies. Rifle companies were organized into a weapons platoon and three rifle platoons. The latter typically consisted of three squads, each with a 7.62mm RPD light machine gun, RPG-2 or RPG-7 (B40, B41) rocket-propelled grenade launchers, 7.62mm AK-47 assault rifles, and possibly a captured 40mm M79 grenade launcher. The weapons platoon would have a few 7.62mm SGM machine guns, two to four 60mm Chinese Type 31 or 63 mortars, and sometimes a couple of 57mm recoilless rifles. There simply was no standard allocation. It was common for captured, US-made, crew-served weapons to be employed, including the 57mm M18A1 and 75mm M20 recoilless rifles (from which the Chinese Types 36 and 52 were copied), 60mm M2 and M19 mortars, and 81mm M1 and M29 mortars.

VC Main Force units were organized in a similar manner to their NVA counterparts, though sometimes were more lightly armed. VC Local Force and Self-Defense units were irregularly organized with a great deal of variation in structure and armament, and as a result any attempt to depict a "standard" table of organization is pointless. There were few crew-served weapons, and small arms were often captured-US, French, or Chinese-supplied foreign weapons, or even homemade arms.

Defensive principles

The key VC/NVA defensive doctrine at lower levels specified that units were to avoid contact if at all possible. They did not normally plan to hold ground and fight off repeated assaults. There were instances where they did this – Hamburger Hill in 1969 for example – but even then they had no intention of retaining a hold on the hill for an extended period. When they did fight for a piece of ground it was often to distract Free World forces from other developments and to tie them down. In other instances it appeared they were merely testing the resolve and capabilities of Free World forces to see if a change in tactics might be in order. In some instances an NVA defensive effort resulting in a prolonged engagement would be an attempt to wear down the enemy. When engaged in their base camps and defended villages, more often than not discovered quite by accident by Free World forces, the VC/NVA would strive to break contact as soon as possible while still inflicting significant casualties on the attackers.

The defensive positions were laid out to confuse and delay attackers. Bunkers and fighting positions were not laid out in orderly geometric patterns, and were intentionally sited in unexpected locations. Some positions were on indefensible terrain, deep within a densely vegetated area, a bolder-strewn ravine, or on a saddle between two dominating hills. To those still burdened with a rigid military mindset and unable to adapt to unconventional asymmetric warfare this seemed inefficient and impractical. It served its purpose to confuse and delay, but also increased the attackers' sense of being engaged from all sides and surrounded, the ideal psychological impression to impart.

A few bunkers and fighting positions would be placed some distance from the main defenses, often appearing to be poorly sited. These might consist of either just one position or a small cluster. Lookout posts (*bai quam sát*) would also be established on trails and other routes leading into occupied areas, on the ground or in trees. The VC/NVA would also post lookouts on potential helicopter landing zones (LZ). These might be teenage villagers. Free World units sometimes approached defended areas on what they thought would be unexpected routes and encountered these scattered positions. Perimeter bunkers would be scattered in irregular lines with apparent gaps. The gaps might be covered by positions further within the perimeter and on the flanks. In other parts of the perimeter the bunkers would be encountered in tight clusters, acting as strongpoints within the main perimeter. With the exception of some of the outlying positions, bunkers were mutually supporting, being covered by flanking positions and others to the rear. To attack one bunker drew fire from other directions. There might be additional interior bunker clusters or defensive lines crisscrossing the perimeter. A two-line defense was standard, featuring an outer perimeter (which in the case of a village might be well outside it) and an inner one (which would be inside the village). This took advantage of the Free World requirement that permission had to be granted by higher headquarters to use artillery and air within 1,000m of populated areas – causing delays to the Free World attack and allowing the VC/NVA time to slip away. They might stay and fight and even counterattack to retake the first line – a technique known as "rubber banding." Trenches, and sometimes tunnels or covered trenches, would link perimeter sectors and clusters, but it was rare for *all* bunkers and positions to be interconnected, as is so often reported by attackers. Trenches and tunnels were used to move reinforcements to threatened sectors, launch counterattacks

An ammunition cache in an NVA base area discovered by Special Forces. The olive drab Chinese ammunition crates are stowed in a pit protected by a thatched roof shelter. The site consisted of a few dozen irregularly scattered shelters containing ammunition and weapons.

A soldier checks the entrance to an NVA bunker for booby traps, while an M60-armed machine gunner stands guard. The roof is made of multiple layers of 3in.-diameter bamboo, which offered good resistance to artillery impacts.

from other sectors, resupply ammunition, and allow concealed withdrawal, all relatively well protected from small arms and artillery fire and air strikes. Though scarce, field telephones were used to maintain communications between key positions within the perimeter.[1] The phone wires were run in drainage ditches, trenches, and tunnels, or otherwise were buried.

All positions were well camouflaged, making it difficult to locate them even when they opened fire. In addition, so many automatic weapons were fired by both sides from different directions that it was almost impossible to locate a position by sound. Some positions, especially well-camouflaged spiderholes, would remain silent until the attackers passed and would open fire from the rear and flanks, sometimes not revealing themselves for a considerable time after action was initiated. The VC/NVA also counted on US forces making a major effort to recover those wounded during the initial combat phase. Rather than pressing the attack, the Americans would lay down a base of fire and make major efforts to recover casualties. The enemy would wait for rescuers to expose themselves and would tie down the attack. Medics[2] were often fired on; for this reason they ceased wearing Geneva Convention crosses and carried rifles to protect their patients and themselves.

Hill and ridge defenses could comprise line after line of bunkers and/or trenches following a feature's contours. Irregular lines were common, as were scattered clusters. Bunkers would be sited to fire down both draws and ridge fingers to catch troops moving up either way. The head of a draw invariably held a bunker. Defensive lines would be found on the reverse slopes, not only to protect the rear and flanks, but to serve as additional lines through which the attacker would have to fight his way downhill to clear the high ground. Infiltrators would invariably work their way in behind the attackers as they reached the crest and fought their way down.

The VC/NVA would also conduct a mobile area defense. Free World forces often committed one to three battalions to an operation, depending on the assessed size of the VC/NVA force in the area. The Free World battalions, once inserted in an LZ, would break into companies and sweep their assigned areas.

[1] Chinese Type 65, Type 65-1, and 0743 plus captured US TA-1/PT and TA-312/PT telephones.
[2] The Army used medical aidmen and the US Marines medical corpsmen.

Three companies, moving slowly in columns, could cover only so much ground in the rugged dense terrain. A VC/NVA battalion in the area would break up into companies and then platoons to spread out over a wide area, larger than could be covered by the Free World units. They might avoid contact, but in some cases they would conduct hit-and-run attacks from different directions on the moving Free World companies. This gave the impression that the VC/NVA force was larger than it actually was and prevented higher headquarters from effectively assessing enemy locations, movements, and intentions. Existing local base camps and defensive positions might be used if they were in the right place. Various obstacles and booby traps would be emplaced, time permitting. They would not let themselves become decisively engaged though; they would hit and run, breaking contact and moving in a different direction to their original route.

Whenever possible, contact was initiated at close range, frequently at a distance of 10–30m, and without warning – effectively an ambush. This close-range engagement served to increase the shock effect, positioned the unit for hugging tactics, negated Free World long-range weapons, and limited their ability to maneuver. Precisely when the VC/NVA would break contact depended on the advantage they held, the Free World reaction (artillery and air support, commitment of reaction forces), the proximity of friendly units, the terrain, and other factors. A rear guard remained in contact with the enemy as the main body withdrew in stages by subunit. The rear guard would spread out through the defended area in an effort to deceive the attackers, before withdrawing in the dark and confusion.

If the VC/NVA became pinned down – closely engaged and unable to disengage without suffering heavy casualties – they would fight until darkness fell and then withdraw on reconnoitered routes to pre-planned rally points, which might possess their own defensive positions, trenches, and bomb shelters plus cached supplies and ammunition. Sappers or other patrols might reconnoiter possible escape routes if not already selected, or might check that routes were free of the enemy. Sapper patrols from outside the contested area might be sent in to locate escape routes and contact the defending unit.

This bamboo framework was part of an NVA bunker. It covered an open fighting position adjacent to the bunker.

Construction techniques and materials

The VC/NVA built extensive tunnel complexes, designed field fortifications, made maximum use of the terrain for cover and concealment, employed ingenious obstacles and booby traps, and became masters at camouflage – all using only human hands and for the most part locally available materials.

The VC/NVA were highly mobile forces, but this mobility was largely limited to movement by foot. Trucks and bicycles, the latter reinforced for carrying cargo loads, were used on the Ho Chi Minh Trail network, which stretched from North Vietnam through Laos and Cambodia with branch trails running into the RVN. The quantity of materials that could be shipped south was restricted and limited to essential items that could not be obtained there. Construction materials did not figure among these, except for heavy bridging material and fuel pipelines for use on the trails.

Materials and acquisition

A surprising variety of materials were acquired in the south through capture in combat, battlefield recovery, pilfering by sympathizers, the black market, and local fabrication. "Jungle factories" were operated by local VC and auxiliaries manufacturing individual equipment, crude munitions, explosive and manual booby traps, and punji stakes. Woodcutters were employed to produce "standardized" lengths and diameters of timber for construction purposes. Commercial woodcutters often paid a "war tax" by "donating" a percentage of the wood they cut and even transporting it to where it was needed.

A soldier examines a woven basket used to remove earth. The NVA bunker has a multi-layered bamboo roof and some of its camouflage has been removed. He is in front of the firing port, demonstrating how difficult it was to detect such bunkers.

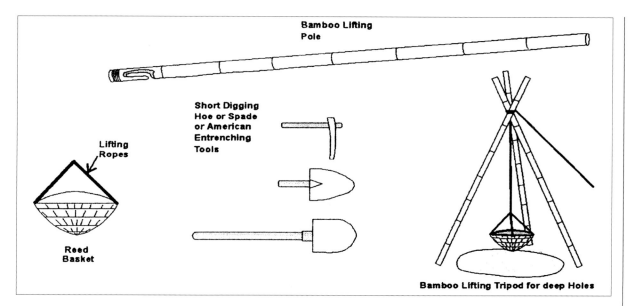

Battlefield recovery and pilfering were important means of acquiring materials and supplies. It was an issue often addressed by Free World units, who were cautioned to remove battlefield litter (American units were particularly lax in this regard), especially at sites such as abandoned firebases. Some units were more conscientious than others, but even a well-disciplined unit could inadvertently leave behind valuable material for the enemy.

Free World fire support bases were temporary in nature. Following closure, the standard procedure was to recover all concertina wire, barbed-wire picket stakes, and field telephone wire; dismantle the many bunkers and artillery positions; collect ammunition boxes and pallets; and bulldoze all trenches, fighting positions, bunkers and weapons pits. Concertina and barbed wire too damaged and tangled to be of further use were bulldozed into trenches and covered over, as were broken pickets and timbers. Sandbags were slit open if overly worn, emptied for reuse, or sling-loaded still full beneath helicopters and flown to a new base for immediate reuse. Bunker materials were recovered, not only to prevent their use by the enemy, but for use in the construction of other firebases – such materials were often in short supply. One mistake made by American forces was to consider bent pickets and airfield matting panels, broken ammunition crates and pallets, and broken timber as unusable: the VC would readily make use of them.

Undamaged construction materials were all too often left in abandoned bases, and carted off by the VC. Periodic harassing artillery fire, booby traps, liberal dustings of CS (tear gas) powder, and stay-behind ambushes did little to discourage VC scavengers. Even munitions, "expended" radio batteries (which in fact retained sufficient energy to detonate a remotely controlled mine), C-rations, and other valuable supplies were taken away. Civilians were often impressed to carry off the recovered materials.

Pilferage and theft were other means of acquiring construction materials. Some materials were diverted when being off-loaded from ships, or removed from contracted trucks en route to Free World bases. Some ARVN officers and civilian contractors were not above selling materials to who they usually thought were other contractors, businessmen, or private individuals obtaining them for their own use; instead, they may well have been VC sympathizers.

Typical materials acquired from Free World sources included dimensioned lumber and timber, plywood, U-shaped steel barbed-wire pickets, wooden cargo pallets, aluminum 88in. × 108in. "speed pallets," wooden ammunition boxes,

A sampling of typical digging implements used by the VC/NVA. The bamboo lifting pole could not practically be much more than 12ft. in length. (Courtesy of Bruce Hanesalo, from *Tunnel Warfare*, Vol. 4)

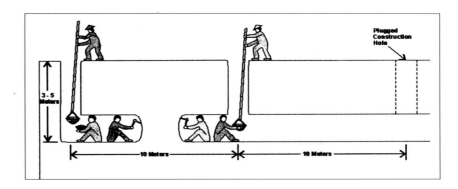

A demonstration of the technique of digging connecting tunnels from multiple excavation shafts, most of which would be filled when completed. (Courtesy of Bruce Hanesalo, from *Tunnel Warfare*, Vol. 4)

metal ammunition cans, tube-like metal artillery powder bag containers, airfield landing mats and pierced steel plates (PSP), 20-gal and 55-gal steel fuel drums (earth-filled), corrugated metal pipe halves, corrugated sheet metal, and plastic and burlap sandbags.[3] Low quality burlap 50kg and 100kg rice bags were also used for sandbags, but they deteriorated quickly. Some use was also made of cinder blocks, bricks, and cement along with dimensioned lumber and corrugated sheet metal diverted from aid supplies provided by government agencies for village reconstruction projects. Railroad rails and ties and steel pipe were also salvaged. Plastic sheeting was widely used for waterproofing roofs. Cloudy semi-translucent plastic sheeting was obtained from US sources. Various types of green plastic sheeting came from the north; one type was light green with a texture similar to crepe paper.

Even though such materials were available, their use was not widespread. Acquisition was difficult, and they could be found in only limited quantities. It was also difficult to move the heavy and bulky materials to where they were needed. Concrete bunkers were occasionally encountered, often with only the roof made of concrete. VC/NVA units and local VC more often than not used what was available – that is, what was provided by nature.

Digging tunnels and building positions

The VC/NVA engaged in much digging, and it was not uncommon for entire units to go underground with their full facilities. Most of the soil in Vietnam was well drained, except in low-lying areas and areas with high water tables, notably along the coast and the Mekong Delta. The geology of the land varied greatly. In the mountains, including those of the piedmont area, granite was common, and limestone was also widely encountered; natural caves and ravines could be found in both the piedmont and high mountains, but were more widespread in the former. Coastal areas featured sandy or clay soils; sandstone was found in this region, and was excellent for tunneling as it required no shoring up. A common soil was laterite, a reddish-brown, hard soil rich in iron oxide. It is created from weathered rock with the silica leached out by water passing through it, particularly in areas of good drainage, and is found in many areas of Vietnam. Laterite was difficult to dig through, but provided good support for tunnels, trenches, and bunker pits. Broken up, it had a coarse gravel-like texture. When used for concrete it required a higher percentage of cement than normal sand and aggregate mixtures, and was less resistant to weathering and wear. Positions were also built out of rocks in mountainous areas, but these were at risk of creating splinters when struck by gunfire. Rocks did have the advantage of being easily blended into the surrounding features though.

Hardwood trees were abundant, including mahogany, ebony, teak, ironwood, eucalyptus, and mangrove, among others. These woods made

---

[3] Descriptions and dimensions of these materials are found in Osprey Fortress 33: *Special Forces Camps in Vietnam 1961–70*.

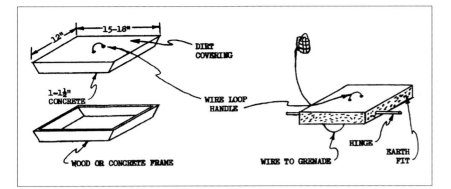

Two common types of tunnel trapdoors, the beveled drop-in type (left) and the hinged concrete one (right), the latter rigged with a booby-trapped hand grenade. The beveled type could be of solid concrete (above) or be made of a wooden frame and bottom and filled with camouflaging earth (below).

excellent heavy construction materials, particularly mahogany and ebony, which are strong and durable. Teak is even harder and has long been used in shipbuilding. Ironwood is strong too, but although it splits and warps when dried, it was used extensively as pole wood. Eucalyptus is a medium hardwood, but is resistant to termites. Mangrove (*Cây Nân*) wood was widely used for house building and does well in a wet environment; it was only found in coastal areas though. Pine (*Thong*) was found in the central plateau and some other highland areas, but has limited strength and deteriorates rapidly. Palm trees were common along the coast, but little used for construction. Relatively easy to cut down, the interior is soft and fibrous, helping them absorb the impact of projectiles, and reducing the risk of splinter wounds. With age and wetness though, coconut logs became spongy, were easily penetrated by projectiles, and lost their ability to support heavy loads. Rubber trees were little used for construction owing to the sticky, smelly sap. Uncured hard- and softwoods deteriorated rapidly in the tropics and were prone to termite attack. Nipa palm, with large fronds divided into long narrow leaflets, provided the most common thatch material.

Bamboo was abundant and widely used for all forms of construction, including houses and furniture. It is flexible in long lengths and rigid in shorter lengths, especially when lashed and cross-braced. A 2in.-diameter section is surprisingly strong. A hollow bamboo stalk is compartmented into sections separated by a fibrous membrane. This can be punched through when a hollow tube is needed. Its diameter can be that of a finger or several inches. Bamboo is extremely dense and hard. Positions were sometimes built inside thickets to deflect small-arms fire.

Strong, flexible, woody vines were used for lashing structures and assemblies. Narrow parallel lengthwise cuts were made on certain types of bamboo stalk, peeled off in long strips, and used for bindings. These natural materials were quite durable, but wire, including recovered field telephone wire, cord, and rope were also used.

Construction principles

The typical Vietnamese peasant farmer, whether from North or South Vietnam, was adept at building structures using local materials and techniques handed down for generations. City dwellers, on the other hand, were poorly skilled in this regard except in wielding hand tools and carrying spoil. The same applied to camouflage: many rural people had a natural eye for blending fortifications into the vegetation and terrain.

The simple construction techniques used to build houses and other rural structures were seen in fortifications and shelters. Split-bamboo, thatching, rough-cut planks, corrugated steel, and dried mud were used in the construction of walls. Thatching, red clay tile, and corrugated steel were used for the roofs. In low-lying areas prone to flooding (in the Delta and on the coastal fringe) houses

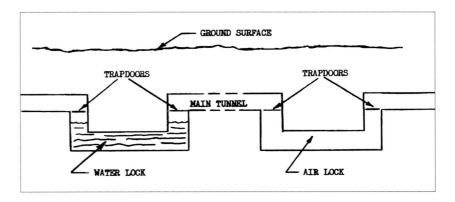

Examples of tunnel water locks and air locks. These halted blast concussion, tear gas, and smoke. They were also time-consuming to construct and restricted air circulation. Tunnel rats were understandably reluctant to negotiate locks as they might be booby-trapped or an ambush might be awaiting them.

were built on stilts, and this also was the case on hillsides. Furniture was also largely made of bamboo and locally cut boards and poles.

Construction techniques varied widely based on the previous experience of the troops, individual preferences, innovation, available time and materials, terrain and vegetation, soil composition, water table, and so on. The construction examples described below are typical, but should not be regarded as ideal examples.

The preference was to build deep below ground with well-supported overhead cover for protection from artillery and air attack. A basic principle was for fighting positions to have at least a portion of themselves covered. The same applied to protective bunkers, shelters and accommodation.

At least two feet of overhead cover was typically used, but as little as 8–10in. might be encountered. Shelter and accommodation bunker roofs were kept flush with the ground if at all possible, but a fighting bunker's roof was required to be above ground to accommodate firing ports. Often bunker pits were narrow, with the short roofing logs running lengthwise and abutting one another. Logs from 3in. to 10in. in diameter were used as well as 2in. or larger bamboo shafts. This required little additional support, but in larger bunkers vertical support posts were used. Gaps between logs were filled with sticks, leaves, and grass. If the roof was flush with the ground the bunker pit was dug deep – a cut-and-fill construction. A wider pit was dug 2ft. or deeper, up to 6ft. on occasions, and the roofing logs placed over the main pit with the logs resting on the wider lips. Two or more layers of logs were sometimes used and were laid crisscrossed in alternating layers. Thick layers of hard-packed clay were also used as overhead cover. If available a layer of sandbags or rocks was laid on top of the logs of thick roofs. The backfill was tamped by foot and log rams. Waterproofing materials consisted of overlapping palm fronds, woven grass mats, layers of bamboo shucks (which also cushioned any blast impact), cardboard (salvaged US C-ration cases were made of semi-water-resistant, heavy-duty, corrugated cardboard), plastic and nylon sheeting, corrugated steel, or a layer of clay. Waterproofing also prevented dirt from falling into the position. The crosswise logs of above-ground roofs were usually supported by lengthwise logs, and the above-ground sidewalls made of stacked logs externally banked with packed earth.

Firing ports were generally small in terms of height and width, to make them difficult to target with gunfire and grenades. Such ports were at ground level or a few inches above it. After-action reports often state that bunkers had 360-degree fields of fire, but this was seldom true: few bunkers had more than one or two ports. The impression of 360-degree fire was given by the presence of mutually supporting bunkers and positions. Fighting bunkers with a port on each side did exist, but were not common.

Entrances and exits to positions were very small, just large enough for a man with a light build to crawl though, once again to make them difficult to locate and hit. In larger bunkers there might be two entrances. One entrance would lead directly into the bunker and the other would connect to a short tunnel. Exits were often configured and situated so that they could be used for firing from. If an entrance trench was present (usually connecting the bunker with a communication or fighting trench) it would typically have a 90-degree turn to protect the occupant from blasts and grenades. The floor was often covered with a layer of leaves, palm fronds, or grass mats if used as an accommodation bunker. In areas with high water tables or poor drainage, or in leaking bunkers, a drainage sump would be dug in the floor to collect water, which could be bailed out. Grenade sumps were also dug. A small dugout hole just large enough for a man might be cut into the inside wall of a bunker for additional protection. Small bunkers might have an air vent in case the entrance was blocked by blast debris.

Bamboo mats were very common. These were made in varying widths and lengths by weaving lengths of split bamboo through three parallel poles. They were used for hut sidewalls, tabletops, sleeping platforms, walkways for muddy trails, and so on.

The A-frame shelter, called a "tepee" bunker by the Americans, was less common. A trench was dug and a log (or a lashed bundle of small poles) was laid lengthwise down the center of the trench with its ends on the trench's end lips. Shorter poles and logs were stacked at an angle on either side. The trench on either side was backfilled to above the roof's peck and then a layer of logs was laid horizontally over this and covered with the remaining earth to create a low mound. The entrance comprised a short, downward-angled, 45-degree slot on one end.

Though commonly found, bomb craters were seldom used as bases for fortifications. They were conspicuous from the air and much of the surrounding vegetation would have been blown away, stripping the area of concealment. However, smaller craters around which vegetation had quickly re-grown were sometimes used. Larger craters were too great in diameter to cover. Additionally, older craters would be shallower than newer ones, owing to rain washing in the sides. In the rainy season (and sometimes even in the dry season, depending on the water table) craters would flood, which provided a source of water in areas devoid of streams. Indeed, water-filled craters made good bathing holes, although the author can attest that despite the surface water being warmed by the sun, a foot beneath it remained chilled. The following table gives a rough estimation of the relation between the size of bomb and the resulting crater (although fuzing, the angle of impact, the thickness of intervening trees, and soil density could all affect this):

Diameter	Depth	Bomb weight
10ft.	5ft.	250 lb.
15ft.	8ft.	500 or 750 lb.
38ft.	20ft.	1,000 or 2,000 lb.

Powered construction equipment was extremely rare in fortification construction. The little equipment that was available (bulldozers and graders) were used on the Ho Chi Minh Trail. Hand tools included long- and short-handle shovels, Chinese and US entrenching tools, pick-mattocks, axes, hoes, trowels, wood saws, two-man crosscut saws, machetes, and buckets and woven baskets with rope handles for hauling earth. For tunneling, shovels, picks, and hoes would have the handles cut short, and tin cans, bowls and scoops were also used. Often tools were in short supply. One NVA prisoner described building a four-man bunker using only a small crosscut saw and a pick; no shovels were available. The pick's pointed end was used to break up the ground and the wider mattock end was used to lift out the spoil – a lengthy process.

An end view cross-section of a typical cut-and-fill-type bunker – essentially a slit trench with two or more layers of crisscrossed logs and backfilled to create overhead cover level with the ground.

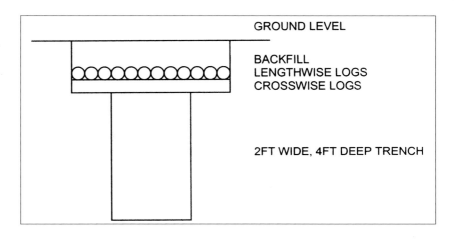

GROUND LEVEL

BACKFILL
LENGTHWISE LOGS
CROSSWISE LOGS

2FT WIDE, 4FT DEEP TRENCH

Simply put, tunneling was slow, hard, grueling labor. Spoil was placed in baskets and pulled to the entry shaft and carted off some distance or dumped in a river. Even a small tunnel system generated a great deal of spoil and it could not be left near the tunnel site. One tunneling method was to dig a series of 2–5m-deep vertical shafts every 10m or so. Two tunneling teams would work in opposite directions from each shaft toward the neighboring shafts. With each team digging only 5m in each segment a tunnel could be completed relatively quickly. Most shafts would be backfilled, and some had bamboo air vents installed. This was impractical for deep tunnels and multi-level systems, where the spoil had to be carried down long shafts and then to the surface. For shallow tunnels a long bamboo pole with a notch in one end was used to lift spoil baskets out of the shaft. Deep tunnels required a bamboo tripod erected over the shaft and baskets hoisted using a rope and pulley.

Everyone in a village was involved in tunneling. Young men and women formed 4–5-person tunneling teams. One dug, one hauled spoil back to the shaft, and the others hoisted it out. They rotated duties frequently. Other teams disposed of the spoil and others cut wood for supports. Old men made spoil baskets and air vents, and repaired tools, while the older women cooked and cared for small children. Children collected camouflage materials, delivered support timbers, and ran errands. A worker was expected to remove 0.5–1 cubic meters of spoil a day depending on age, health, soil density, weather, and the like. Families were assigned specific tunnel sections to maintain.

Camouflage

Although camouflaging fortifications is a fairly standard procedure, it was absolutely essential for the VC/NVA. The best-built fortifications and shelters were worthless if they were detected, and the Free World forces possessed many reconnaissance and surveillance assets. If they could be seen, they could (and probably would) be destroyed.

The first layer of protection afforded the VC/NVA was the overhead canopy of the forests, dense brush, bamboo, and high grass. Even scout helicopters hovering just above trees, or occasionally dropping down in natural clearings, had great difficulty detecting enemy activity and structures. Double- and triple-canopy jungle was almost impossible to see into, as was the dense single canopy of rubber plantations. Underbrush and bamboo provided an additional layer of protection. After the 1968 siege of Khe Sanh was lifted NVA positions and base camps were reconnoitered on the ground and their location precisely determined. Subsequent low-altitude air reconnaissance still could not detect them.

Fortifications were blended and contoured into the terrain and vegetation. The fact that most structures were made of natural materials made them even more difficult to detect. They were hidden in hedgerows, tree lines, bamboo thickets, clumps of brush, and along stream and gulley banks. Trenches might be roofed with palm fronds, tree limbs, grass, or reeds for concealment. For additional protection small logs roofed some trench sections and were covered with earth.

Bunkers were kept as low as possible to the ground, and firing ports and entrances were kept small. They were seldom dug beneath large trees because of the presence of roots. In areas with houses on stilts they

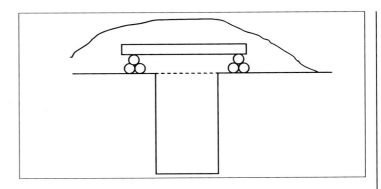

An end view cross-section of a small, simple bunker with above-ground overhead cover. This allowed a firing port to be constructed in the sidewall. The sidewall logs would be staked in place on both sides.

were prepared below the structure, hiding them in the shadows of the building. "Spiderholes" were dug in high grass and brush and fitted with lifting lids made of small limb frames camouflaged with grass, vines, and twigs. Fighting positions and hideouts were prepared within abandoned termite mounds and haystacks.

Ground-cover materials and sods were carefully removed before excavation began, and once the position was completed they were replaced. Sometimes the ground was wetted down to make the removal of the upper layer easier. Small plants were often planted on the tops and sides of earth-covered positions and watered. Care was taken to ensure transplanted vegetation matched that found in the immediate area, to ensure it blended in well. In a matter of weeks the tropical vegetation would flourish around the position, adding to the camouflage. Efforts were made to reduce the presence of trampled grass and disturbed vegetation; the VC/NVA were good about removing or disguising all signs of work in an area. Free World forces were seldom forewarned when they entered a defended area.

Removed spoil was spread beneath dense vegetation and covered with leaves away from trails, or dumped in streams, ponds, fresh or water-filled bomb craters, or spread on roads, cultivated fields or bare ground within the hamlet. Because of the quantity and weight of spoil it was seldom carried far, often only c.30m or less in some cases. Parapets and other exposed soil were covered with leaves, elephant grass, palm fronds, or reeds. The VC/NVA were very much aware that freshly turned soil appeared as white against gray in aerial photographs. Wood-cutting areas were supposed to be one-hour's walk (about three miles) from the camp or defensive position but they were often much closer. In the 1st Infantry Division's area of operations they were almost certain to find a camp within 200–500m of a wood-cutting site.

Machine gun fire-lanes were carefully cleared through dense vegetation. Only selected low vegetation was removed along with the lower limbs of bushes. Trees, saplings, larger bushes and the like were kept in situ. Free World troops would be unaware they had entered a field of fire, and that their boots were visible to enemy gunners at ground level.

"Poorly camouflaged" dummy positions were sometimes constructed to draw air and artillery fire away from the main base camp or defensive position.

Discipline and control measures were also part of camouflage. This included limiting movement, even that of individuals, as well as noise, light, fire, cooking, and litter discipline. The VC/NVA were usually effective in these, but their weakest point was light discipline when moving at night – for fear of snakes.

Secrecy was another factor. Often villagers built bunkers and tunnels, emplaced booby traps, closed entrances, and placed camouflage. While many were sympathizers, others were forced laborers. Their "loyalty" was ensured by making it perfectly clear what would happen to them and their families if it faltered, often by explicit demonstrations in village meetings.

Field fortifications

This category of fortifications includes individual fighting positions, crew-served weapons positions, fighting and protective bunkers, and trenches. The dimensions provided in the text that follows are typical ones, and may have varied – as did the construction methods between units.

There was no formal fortification manual, but guidelines were published in the form of a ten-page directive, which was captured in late 1967 but not translated and distributed to Free World forces until early 1969. These guidelines offered precise guidance on site selection, construction steps and procedures, camouflage techniques and the like, but offered no standardized designs or dimensions, although the tunnel booklet did give tunnel dimensions (0.8–1.2m wide, 0.8–1.5m high). Some fortifications were based on Chinese and Soviet practices. Chinese experiences from the Korean War did offer some valuable insights, but most of the Korean War witnessed static warfare in barren hills, in hot dry summer and freezing winter conditions. The Chinese endured massive artillery barrages heavier than the VC/NVA normally had to face and kept entire divisions underground. Little of this was of use to the VC/NVA, who had been developing their own fortification and tunneling techniques during the war with France at the same time the Chinese were facing UN forces. They did a good job of adapting and developing fortifications to suit their needs, the terrain, and the strategic situation.

Simple, hasty fighting positions included small circular or square holes dug to a depth that allowed the fighter to sit, kneel, or stand. A short slit trench might be used, which could accommodate two or three men. Shallow prone shelters just large enough for a man to lie in were used as hasty or overnight shelters. These would be found along trails and in temporary camps. The most common was the L-shaped hole. A 2ft.-diameter circular hole was dug down 4ft. or more and a 3ft.-high, 2ft.-wide niche was dug 3ft. deep into the side allowing a man to squat in the hole and be reasonably protected from artillery, aerial rockets, and the like. Some form of camouflage cover was provided, either a latticework "spiderhole" cover of woven grass, tree limbs, an uprooted clump

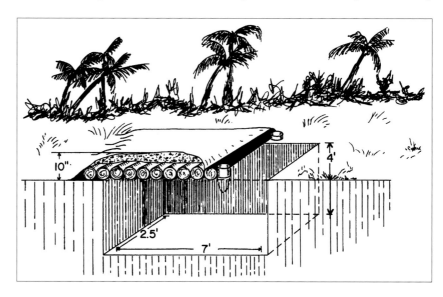

An individual fighting/living bunker as found outside Khe Sanh. The open end doubled as a firing position and entry. The roofing logs were held in place by stakes.

This common type of living bunker at Khe Sanh was covered by two layers of crisscrossed logs, earth, and rocks. Note the slanting entry "tunnel." The niche dug in the side measured 8in. × 12in. × 12in.

of brush, or palm fronds. Small protective positions were encountered holding two or thee men. These were generally 3ft. wide, 4ft. deep, and 6ft. long.

Along canal or river banks, small one-man holes were dug from which to execute ambushes. Hidden among brush, the openings were well camouflaged. A crawl tunnel could lead down to water level for escape, hidden among aquatic plants. Examples of two-man fighting positions included a 6–10ft. trench covered by 10–12in. of logs and earth, and a 2ft.-diameter tunnel, often running as much as 4ft. beneath the brush or bamboo above so that the roots would reinforce the roof; a 2ft.-diameter fighting hole would be located at either end.

Trenches were seldom dug in angular, geometric patterns with turns made at regular intervals (something that characterized Free World trenches). VC/NVA trenches were serpentine, following the terrain contours and running through the densest vegetation to make airborne detection difficult. They would make a direction change every 10–25ft. Trenches and other open-topped positions normally had the spoil removed for concealment purposes, rather than using it to build parapets. Parapets were built if time did not allow deeper trenches to be dug, if the ground was too hard, or if the water table was too high. Trenches were narrow, only 18–24in. wide, for improved protection and to make detection difficult. They could be wider, depending on their purpose, especially if crew-served weapons were to be moved through them. Their depth varied greatly, but 4ft. was typical; they were deeper in more exposed areas, and only 2ft. deep if used as crawl trenches.

A local VC unit often prepared numerous hiding holes around the village complex from which it operated, both within hamlets (in all sorts of ingenious places) and outside of them. They might be individually located or in clusters of two to four some 10–30m apart. When a Free World force approached they would either hide and await their departure or they might emerge individually and in small numbers to harass, lay booby traps, observe their actions, and hide if chased. There were significantly more hiding holes than fighters in a unit, and a great deal of care and concealment effort went into creating these. They could hold between one and six people, and were located in bamboo and brush thickets; in stream and ditch banks; inside haystacks, piled up dead trees, or pig pens; beneath manure piles; within cemeteries; and countless other places, especially those which soldiers would not care to search. One form was a simple cave-like hollow for one to eight men barely above the waterline inside the bank of a river, stream, or pond. A small tunnel was concealed at the waterline or below it.

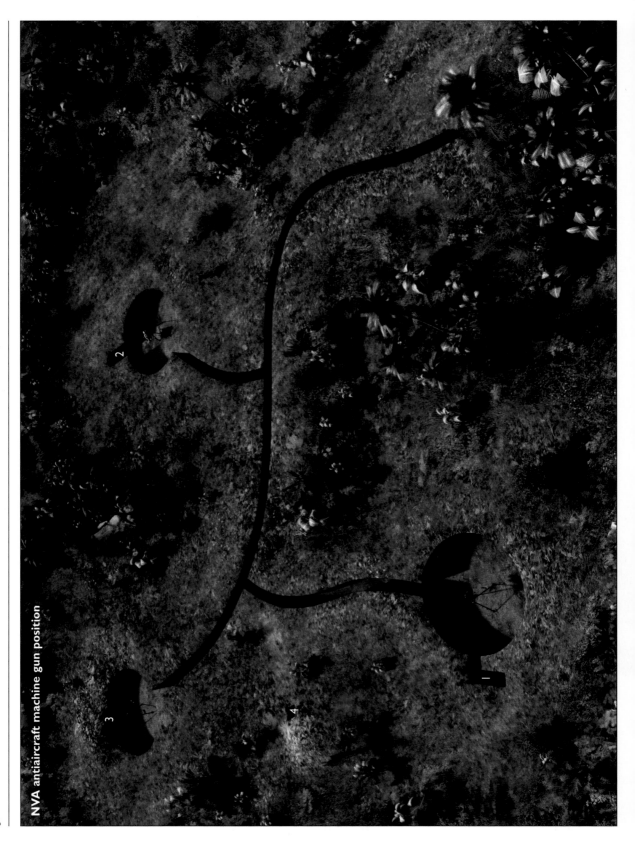

The Soviet-made 12.7mm DShKM38/46 and its Chinese-made version, the Type 54, were the primary AA weapons employed by VC/NVA units in the RVN. In order to intensify the concentration of fire against helicopters and fast-moving fighter-bombers, the three guns of an AA machine gun platoon were positioned in close proximity to one another. All three weapons normally engaged the same aircraft. This permitted centralized fire control, the easier replacement of casualties, and a more efficient resupply and redistribution of ammunition. Gun pits were typically 9ft. in diameter and 4ft. deep. Either a small L-shaped trench (1), its arms 4ft. and 6ft. long, or a 6ft.-long straight slit trench (2) were dug in the side. Both were 2–3ft. wide and covered with a layer of 3in. logs and up to 3ft. of earth and rocks (removed here for clarity on two of the pits, but shown in place at 3). These were for immediate cover if attacked, as well as for ready ammunition storage. Some pits had an 8in.-high, 2ft.-diameter earth platform on which ammunition boxes were placed beneath the tripod. A 4ft.-deep, 4ft.-wide, 6ft.-long earth-covered command bunker (4) is located nearby. Besides triangular positions they were also emplaced in a linear pattern, especially on ridge tops. At Khe Sanh three-gun positions protected mortar platoons and were found on hills and ridges protecting base camps and storage sites. Single-gun positions were scattered about living areas, trench complexes, and along supply routes. In this illustration, camouflage has been removed from the entire position to show it more clearly.

Crew-served weapons positions were simple. There were no complex designs as is so common in Western field fortifications. Light and heavy machine guns (bipod- and tripod-mounted, respectively) were fired from one- or two-man fighting holes or bunkers altered to accommodate them; an earth platform was provided for the tripod. Recoilless rifles/guns were fired from shallow open pits, often with camouflaged parapets to the sides, but more commonly from behind any available cover. The only requirement was for a clear area to the rear for the back-blast. Positions were often built under a tree to conceal them from the air and help hide the back-blast signature. RPG-2s and RPG-7s were also fired in the open without prepared positions, usually from behind a tree, and also required a clear back-blast area. DKZs and RPGs created significant flash, smoke, and dust signatures, but were repositioned frequently, negating the need for complex positions.

Mortar positions were usually circular and just large enough to accommodate the mortar and its two- to four-man crew. The depth might be 2–4ft. with a diameter of 4–5ft. for the 60mm, 6–7ft. for the 82mm, and 8–9ft. for the 120mm mortar. There might be a covered short slit or L-shaped trench to the side for ammunition storage, and smaller "ready" ammunition niches might be dug into the sidewall. To support an attack or siege, a mortar platoon's three or four positions might be connected by communication trenches leading to the rear, where the command post and ammunition storage were located. The pits were typically arranged in a staggered line. Out of necessity, mortars were required to be in the open so were well camouflaged with the soil removed. For additional concealment they were often prepared in areas of brush or high grass, which was pulled over the position. Woven grass mats provided additional camouflage. During prolonged occupation the pits would be dug deep and made as small as possible, as they would have to resist air strikes. Deep protective/living bunkers would branch off the communication trenches.

Antiaircraft (AA) positions for 12.7mm DShKM38/46 machine guns also used circular pits 9ft. in diameter and 4ft. deep. They too had covered slit and L-shaped trenches to the sides. An AA platoon had three guns and the positions were placed 30–60ft. apart in a triangle connected by trenches. The trenches did not run from

An L-shaped living bunker at Khe Sanh, which could accommodate four men. The overhead cover was substantial. The sandbags were obtained from an overrun Free World installation in Khe Sanh Village. Such bunkers could have a slanted entry "tunnel" plus, in some cases, an escape tunnel.

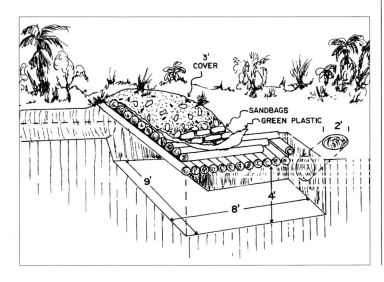

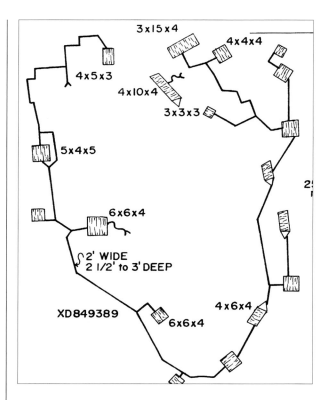

This living bunker complex at Khe Sanh is a good example of the wide variety in bunker dimensions, largely based on individual preference. The triangular bunkers are of the "teepee" type. The connecting trenches were shallow crawl trenches without parapets. The position was concealed within an area of dense brush and high grass, and housed 40–60 men.

position to position, but a single long serpentine trench ran between the two positions to the third. Branch trenches connected the two side positions to the main trench. The distance between the individual positions varied in order to provide a less recognizable pattern. Communications trenches connecting crew-served weapons positions provided protected access to bunkers when artillery and air strikes arrived, as well as facilitating the supply of ammunition and replacement of casualties. At Khe Sanh an AA machine gun platoon protected each nearby mortar platoon. During sieges, an AA position might consist of a 12.7mm gun pit connected by a c.10ft.-long trench to a fighting position with a light machine or just a rifleman's hole to fire on the besieged Free World base. Such a position might be manned by only two or three fighters.

Bunkers (*quân su'* or *boongke* – the latter a Vietnamization of the English term) varied widely in design and purpose: they could be used for fighting, protection, living (or a combination of these), machine gun positions, command posts, signal posts, aid stations, storage for ammunition, rations, supplies, equipment, and other purposes. Bunkers tended to be small, thus requiring only modest materials and less time to build, allowing the wider dispersal of troops, making them easier to conceal during and after construction with less spoil to dispose of, and making them more difficult to detect and target. They typically held two to six men. If there was a "standard" size small bunker, it was 3ft. wide, 4ft. deep, and 6ft. long. There were so many variations that only a small sample can be dealt with below.

An example of a large fighting bunker is a 12–15ft.-square pit with sidewalls built up and a layered roof 2–3ft. above ground. A bunker this size might have a firing port on each side. Such bunkers could also be rectangular with the width a third or half their length. Such bunkers were often situated where their fire could cover large portions of the base camp. This type of bunker was also used as a command post, but might be smaller. One type of protective bunker was a 3ft.-deep, 1.5ft.-wide, 10ft.-long slit trench covered with 2–3ft. of logs and earth with an entrance at one or both ends.

The author encountered a large base camp belonging to the 141st Regiment, 7th NVA Division in Bien Long Province in 1969 near the Cambodian border. The small fighting/living bunkers comprised a 6–8ft.-long, 3ft.-wide, 4ft.-deep slit trench. Short logs were laid crossways atop lengthwise support logs set on the edge of the pit and covered with a foot of red earth. On opposite sides of the ends were 2ft.-square entry openings. These were also used as rifle-firing steps. In some, a small firing port replaced the entry on the side facing the perimeter and others had a shallow downward sloping entrance.

A selection of the wide variety of fighting positions and bunkers found at Khe Sanh serves to demonstrate the lack of standardization. A simple fighting/living bunker consisted of a 4ft.-deep, 2.5ft.-wide, 7ft.-long pit. It was coved by 4in.-diameter logs laid crossways on the ground and covered by 6in. of soil. A 2ft. length at one end was left uncovered from which to fire. Another was 4ft. deep, 4ft. wide, and 6ft. long, and was completely covered by two layers of crisscrossed logs and 2ft. of mounded earth and small rocks. The entrance was a 2ft.-diameter "tunnel" on the side at one end; it was set 2ft. from the side and angled steeply downward into the bunker. L-shaped living bunkers were dug with 9ft. and 8ft. arms, both 4ft. wide and deep. The overhead comprised two crisscrossed layers of 6in. logs overlaid with green plastic sheeting and 3ft. of mounded sandbags, rocks, and earth with brush and grass transplanted on top. The entry was a slanted "tunnel" as used with the previous bunker, but centered on one end of an arm. Over 70 of these bunkers were found in a 200m × 400m area of scrub brush and elephant grass. Many of the bunkers were connected by narrow crawl trenches without parapets. Four men occupied such a bunker and slung their hammocks from roof beams. Other L-shaped fighting/living bunkers were found in the rubber plantation near Khe Sanh Village south of the base. They made use of materials salvaged from civilian and military buildings in the village. These L-shaped bunkers comprised two 6–7ft.-long, 4ft. × 4ft. arms, with only one arm covered by a single layer of logs, boards, or barbed-wire pickets with their edges overlapping. Corrugated steel sheets or green plastic served as waterproofing. Sandbags and earth were piled 3ft. thick. The open arm served as a fighting position; two men occupied such a position.

More elaborate living bunkers were built for long-term occupation. The following bunker design was used by the D-2 Main Force Battalion in Bien Hoa Province near Saigon in 1970. The pit was 12ft. long, 5ft. wide, and 5–6ft. deep. It was covered by a layer of about sixteen 4in.-diameter logs running lengthwise. Their ends rested on the ground and a single crosswise log ran across the center for additional support. They were covered with a sheet of nylon fabric for waterproofing mounded over with 2ft. of earth and camouflaged with transplanted bushes. On opposite sides of one end 2ft. × 3ft. entrances were cut with steps. Saplings were planted around the two entrances and the bunker constructed beneath several large trees. Inside, vertical posts provided additional roof support, with two at each end outset from the walls. Two hammocks were suspended from each pair of posts, one above the other. Other bunkers were 2–3ft. wider and accommodated three pairs of hammocks.

This L-shaped fighting bunker at Khe Sanh consisted of a wider than normal (4ft.) fighting trench and a covered protective bunker, also used as a living bunker. The presence of the entry slot indicates that it may have served to cover the open trench.

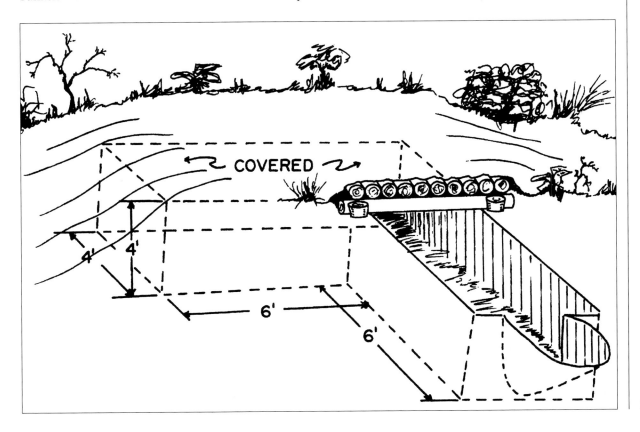

Cutaway of an **NVA** fighting/living bunker

Camps and villages

Base camps

Base camps, which the VC/NVA called "camp sites" (*trai*), were scattered all over remote areas and along trail networks. They were used as rest areas for troops coming from the north or while deploying within the RVN, as long-term bivouacs (in secure areas), as training sites, and as operational staging areas. Rest camps were located on cross-country routes from 8 to 14 hours apart – a night's hard marching. Local units could have any number of small base camps scattered throughout their area. One might be elaborately fortified as a final refuge. Transiting NVA and Main Force units would use some of these, but the local unit would have other secret camps reserved for itself. A camp could be of any size, but usually held a company or battalion and occasionally a regiment. Squad and platoon base camps were also common, allowing the dispersal of larger units. There were scores of independent local VC platoons and while they mostly operated from villages, they maintained several camps to flee to if pressured or to use as patrol bases. These small camps might also be found scattered through areas within several kilometers of Free World bases for use by surveillance and reconnaissance parties.

Besides being located in remote areas, camps were generally placed well away from roads, canals, and navigable rivers. Nearby streams were necessary for water and washing, and camps were often within 150m of a stream, river, or canal. Sometimes the river or canal was integrated into the defensive plan, eliminating an avenue of approach; rice paddies and swamps were used in the same manner. Dense overhead vegetation was essential for concealment; the camps could be located anywhere – on hill and ridge tops or their sides, in valleys, on the flat – but foliage-covered ground was vital. Although a unit would fight from a base camp, it would not fight to keep control of it: the camps were not tactically important and the goal was to avoid fighting the enemy when he had the advantage. They were often placed in terrain where there was only one or two suitable approach routes for large units and defenses and booby traps would be concentrated there. In some areas it was possible to assess where camps might be located. The 1st Brigade, 101st Airborne Division, for example, studied known camps for common positioning factors. It was found that the VC in the area habitually established camps on the upper reaches of draws where water was available along with dense overhead cover. Such sites were plotted on maps and then reports of enemy movements obtained from aerial photos, airborne inferred

LEFT **Cutaway of an NVA fighting/living bunker**
The 141st Regiment, 7th NVA Division used an easily constructed bunker suitable for both fighting and living. Scores of these bunkers were found in a rubber plantation in Bien Long Province in 1969. They comprised 6–8ft.-long, 3ft.-wide, 4ft.-deep slit trenches covered with 1ft.-thick log and earth roofs. On opposite sides of the ends were 2ft.-square entrances. These were also used as rifle-firing steps. In some a firing port replaced the entry on the side facing the perimeter. Two men occupied each bunker. These bunkers were dug on the side of a gently sloping ridge, allowing the firing port to cover the slope. Normally base camps were built in areas of dense foliage. Rubber plantations were devoid of underbrush with trees in orderly rows and a grid of dirt roads. It was assumed that this base camp was constructed here because the rubber trees precluded aerial observation, there were unhindered fields of observation and fire, and because searching Free World units would not expect a base within a plantation. It was in this type of bunker that the author received enemy fire, as mentioned in the text.

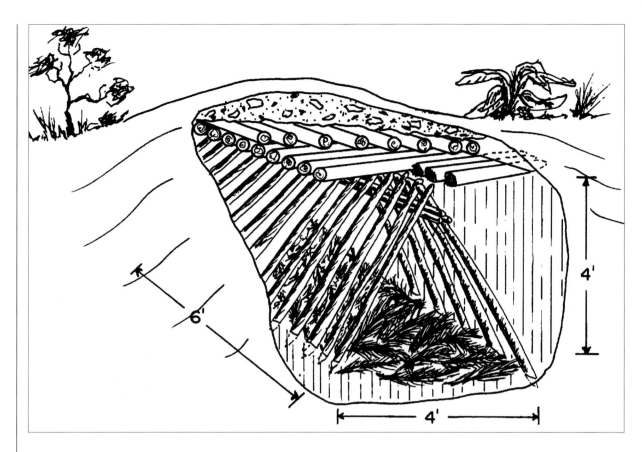

The "teepee" type or "A-frame" bunker was quite resistant to nearby bomb and shell hits, but required more time and materials to construct. The A-frame would have to be covered with material to keep earth from falling in.

sensors ("Red Haze"),[4] airborne side-looking radar, long-range reconnaissance patrols, and special agents were plotted and active camps were often determined.

The camps were very well hidden, far from trails and areas frequented by civilians, who were ordered by the VC to avoid certain locations. They were also protected by lookouts and booby traps, in contrast to temporary VC Main Force and NVA base camps, which were not as well protected. Rest camps and training camps also had limited defenses.

In addition to numerous fighting and living bunkers, the camps contained command posts, signal posts, aid stations, kitchens, storage shelters, above-ground living huts with hammocks or bamboo platform beds, open-sided huts with tables, open-air classrooms, latrines, wash-racks, trash pits, and other facilities. Water was stored in 55-gal steel drums in bunkers or pits, or in open rectangular pits with a log running down the centerline from which was suspended hammock-like plastic sheeting filled with water.

A small command bunker was more or less centrally located along with a signal post. Company command bunkers would be scattered around the perimeter just behind the second-line defenses

Cooking was usually done on a squad basis or in even smaller groups. The small fires produced little smoke, but consumed a great deal of fuel, mainly charcoal, which had to be created and transported. Centralized cooking was more efficient, but required larger fires that made more smoke. The problem had been solved years before by the invention of the Dien Bien Phu stove. A cooking stove

---

[4] "Red Haze" was an AN/UAS-4 or 14 inferred sensor system aboard an OV-1C/D Mohawk capable of detecting vehicle engine heat, camp fires, etc. and recording the readings on film.

was constructed in a bunker or tunnel with a vent over it to draw in air. A narrow slanting tunnel ran upward toward the surface into a small trench, which was covered with small logs and a layer of earth. A couple of larger chambers were spaced along the trench to trap smoke and also serve as sumps to collect rainwater. Along the far end of the trench several bamboo tubes branched off at 90 degrees, with vertical bamboo tubes fitted at the end of the branch tubes. The stovepipes were hidden beneath trees and dense vegetation to disperse the smoke.

Camps were circular or oval in shape. The perimeter followed natural terrain features and bunkers and facilities were sited more for concealment and blending into the terrain and vegetation than for tactical positioning. There was usually a second line of bunkers, perhaps less dense as two platoons manned the company's outer line and one platoon the second, although there might be unmanned bunkers for men falling back from the first line. There would be scattered outlying positions on the approaches. Any mortar positions would be wherever there were overhead openings, but these were seldom emplaced, as by nature camps were built in densely vegetated areas. Kitchens, aid stations, storage bunkers and the like would be in or near the central area, but usually well dispersed. Troops would sleep in hammocks suspended between trees or hung inside bunkers depending on the likelihood of attack. Bamboo or stick sleeping platforms for one to four personnel were often used, because of high water, snakes, and rats.

A company base camp could have up to 60 bunkers and positions and a battalion one perhaps 150. Usually, though, they had far fewer, 30 and 80 for example. They could be spread over an area between 100m and 800m wide, and could also be spread out in clusters over quite large areas. A trail usually ran the length of the camp with branching off trails. Open and covered trenches and tunnels might be present, depending on the camp's purpose and duration of its occupation. Some were quite well developed after prolonged use, being periodically occupied for years.

Base camps could be much smaller, notably those used by independent platoons, as way stations, or as bases for patrols operating in distant areas. The example described below was discovered by the author's Cambodian strike force company some 10km west of the company's Special Forces camp, Chi Linh in Bein Long Province, in 1969. The base camp was probably used by VC patrols keeping Chi Linh under surveillance. There may have been a dozen such camps throughout Chi Linh's 2,500 square km area of operations. A patrolling company could pass within 20–30m of such a camp and not notice it in the dense vegetation. A sharp-eyed Stryker glimpsed some framework through the thick bamboo covering the area. Entering such a camp was risky owing to booby traps and only a small number of the company did so while the rest provided external security.

The camp covered an area only about half the size of a tennis court, which was reasonably clear except for small but high bamboo clumps. The clearing

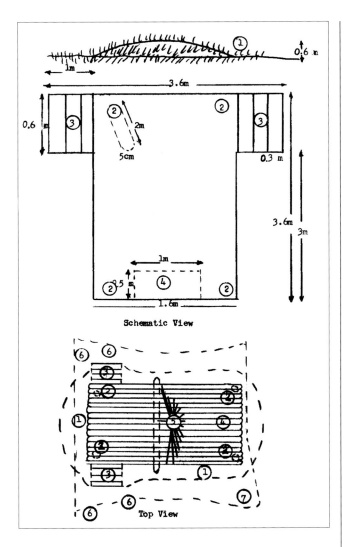

An elaborate four-man living bunker used by D-2 VC Main Force battalion in 1970. (1) 0.6m-thick earth for overhead cover. (2) 2cm-diameter, 2m-high support posts, also used to suspend hammocks. (3) Entrance steps. (4) An equipment storage shelf. (5) Roof logs including a supporting cross log. (6) The edge of a nylon waterproof sheet. (7) A nylon sheet.

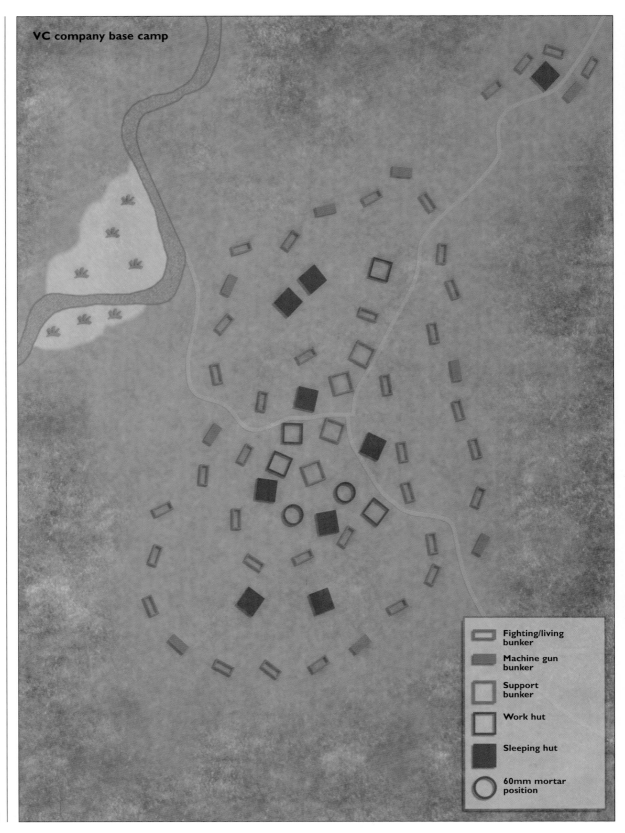

VC company base camp

Fighting/living
bunker

Machine gun
bunker

Support
bunker

Work hut

Sleeping hut

60mm mortar
position

was surrounded by dense bamboo over 30ft. high, which had been bent over, making the camp invisible from the air. The ground in the clearing and all structures were covered with a layer of tan-colored dead bamboo leaves, adding to the camouflage. The facilities were basic, and the centerpiece was a bunker. Because of the risk of booby-trapping it could not be entered and its interior dimensions were only estimated. It was 10–12ft. long, 5–6ft. wide, and 5ft. deep. Roof construction comprised 8in.-diameter logs with about three center support posts and probably similar posts along the sides. The logs were covered by 3ft. of earth above ground level. There were sloping entry trenches about 10ft. long and 3ft. wide leading straight into the bunker from either end. It was strictly a protective shelter, as were the two small slit trenches with parapets on either side of the clearing (3ft. wide, 3ft. deep, 6ft. long). There were no dedicated fighting positions. The camp was not meant to be defended, but served only as a patrol base. The only other structure was an open-sided 8ft. × 10ft. hut. Its thatch roof was supported by six 5in.-diameter posts. A bamboo table with bamboo benches occupied the hut, which was presumably used as an all-purpose structure for meals, meetings, classes, and shelter from the rain. Rub marks on larger bamboo stalks around the clearing's edge indicated up to a dozen men had erected hammocks and ponchos. There were a couple of small fire pits and a clay oven with a hollowed bamboo stack. A filled-in pit-type latrine lay about 20m outside the clearing and a couple of older ones were noted. A trash pile on the edge contained worn-out uniform scraps, tin cans, broken bottles, a few ammunition cans, an AK-47 magazine with a bullet hole, and bits of scrap metal. The trash pile was a source of booby trap materials.

Fortified villages

Defended villages were common in the early days of the war, but as the war escalated and more Free World forces were deployed it became increasingly difficult to fortify villages outright. Sufficient Free World units could now be committed and massive firepower delivered to make a deliberate fixed defense futile. Originally villages were defended to resist government intrusion, an outward show of defiance and the refusal to accept establishment of government authority. If government officials were installed they and their families often experienced brief tenures. Later village defenses were more passive and mainly served to hide the inhabitants or protect them from fire rather than to conduct an outright defense. A VC self-defense force would remain hidden waiting for the Free World force to pass by. If the force was small, the defenders might ambush or harass them outside the village.

As with everything else there was no set pattern or design for a fortified village. It depended on the village/hamlet size, terrain, vegetation, natural obstacles, approach routes, resources, and available manpower (VC and civilian). The general lay of the land and the shape of the defended area were major factors

LEFT **VC company base camp**

VC/NVA base camps could be of any size and shape; the one shown here covers roughly a 100m × 300m area. They were generally oval or circular, which were less than ideal for defensive fire. However, they were more effective for concealment as the layouts followed no recognizable geometric pattern, making it difficult for ground attackers to discern the locations of defensive positions. A base camp would be located entirely beneath trees (removed here for clarity), and would be invisible from the air. The trails were established by the occupants and did not already exist; camps were built well away from established routes. A nearby stream (as a water source) was essential. Each platoon and squad was assigned a defense sector. The second line of bunkers can be discerned in this illustration, and although this was common, for temporary and transient camps this line may not have been established. The bunkers are for the most part two-man fighting/living bunkers. The machine gun bunkers serve the same purpose, but have a light machine gun. The work huts are open-sided and used for weapon cleaning, classes, eating, or storage. The sleeping huts have platform beds. Booby traps would protect the camp's approaches.

for its layout. Lookout posts, local security patrols, small scattered outlying defensive positions, and booby traps on approaches were the first line of defense.

Perimeter defenses consisted of zigzag trenches, small bunkers, and fighting positions, often integrated into existing structures and terrain features. They might be located in vegetation clumps such as bamboo thickets, banana tree stands and hedgerows; inside houses; beneath stilt-houses; within cemeteries and gardens; and along walls and drainage ditches. The main defenses might be positioned outside the village if the terrain and defense forces were adequate. Rivers, streams, canals, ponds, and rice paddies were incorporated into the obstacle plan. Mines and booby traps might be emplaced on approach routes, especially in dense vegetation giving concealment to the attacker (with warnings to villagers to avoid the areas). This might force the attackers to approach on roads or across rice paddies. Interlocking fields of fire would be set up between adjacent hamlets. The few crew-served weapons that were available were widely dispersed between hamlets. Mortars and recoilless rifles might be emplaced on high ground outside the village to fire on approaching Free World forces relying on their stand-off distance to initially protect them. There may or may not have been an internal, second-line defense. It was typically inside the village and there might be traversing trenches connecting different sectors.

The government provided villages with building materials for new and better housing, but some of this was funneled to the VC and used in defensive positions. An incongruity was that the government often assisted with erecting barbed-wire cattle fences around villages and hamlets. Somehow, without a resident defense force, this was supposed to keep out the VC attempting to exploit the villagers for their tax money, food, manpower, and hearts and minds – which it did not. In reality, when Free World troops approaching a village were met by fire they also faced a government-issue barbed-wire fence. Concertina wire and other barbed-wire obstacles were sometimes encountered, as were mines and punji stake belts. Most of the defenses, shelters, and obstacles were built by the villagers, regardless of where their loyalties might actually lie.

The war's reality required every village house to have a bomb shelter. This was a simple, partly sunken dugout, called a "hole" (*Hum*). They were (often) made of government-supplied sandbags, planks, earth-filled fuel drums, and logs with banked earth on the sides and roofs. The bunkers were just large enough for a family. The VC would use these too, in some instances turning out the occupying family. They had only one tiny entrance and no vision ports so they made poor fighting positions. Similar shelters and slit trenches were found along roads outside villages and at the corners of fields for cover from sudden artillery and air attacks. Tunnels were an integral part of village defenses and used to shelter inhabitants, fighters, and supplies, for movement to different sectors, and for escape.

A defended village could be devastated if resistance was shown. The attackers would back off rather than waste casualties in a vicious, close-quarter fight. Artillery, attack helicopters, and fighter-bombers would level the village. Surviving structures were burned as Free World forces swept through to mop up and relocate the surviving villagers to Strategic Hamlets (*Âp Chien-Luoc*) or New Life Hamlets (*Âp Tan Sinh*) in secure areas.

Tunnel systems

The VC were renowned for their extensive use of tunnels (*dào*). Some systems were very small, serving as underground base camps or shelters in which to hide when the enemy searched a village. Others were extremely large and sophisticated, multi-level complexes boasting all the amenities of large surface base camps and extending for thousands of meters. Some of these systems were expanded over a period of years and became quite elaborate. It is often said that the US did not realize the extent of the tunnels, or did not discover them until late in the war, or never discovered many of them. The ARVN was fully aware of the existence of tunnels and US units began discovering them shortly after they arrived in early 1965. By the end of the year techniques had been developed to detect and neutralize tunnels. There were of course small systems that were not discovered or even searched for. Some of the larger systems were not fully explored, nor was it always necessary to do so. However, it is true that the extent of the interconnection of some systems was not realized. The Cu Chi system, for example, was never fully revealed.

The minimum tunnel depth was about 4ft., and few were more than 40ft. deep. Long tunnel courses could be straight or winding, but were more commonly zigzagged at 60–120-degree angles at irregular intervals. Often tunnels were slightly inclined so seepage would collect in shallow sumps dug at intervals, to be pumped or bailed out: a level tunnel could easily flood. Even so, during the rainy season some tunnels might have to be abandoned. The sumps or water traps could be deep pits or U-shaped bends in the floor (four 90-degree turns). A person would have to duck into it and crawl through a flooded chamber for several feet. Water traps also blocked blast overpressure from traveling down a tunnel and were sometimes dug near entrances. Dry traps served the same purpose. These traps also blocked the spread of tear gas and smoke. Horizontal tunnel sections might make a sharp turn near an entry shaft to reduce blast effects. A blast chamber, a short dead-end tunnel, might be dug at these turns.

Tunnel cross-sections were typically 0.8–1.2m wide and 0.8–1.5m high (2.5–3.9ft wide, 2.6–4.9ft high), tending toward the smaller, with an arched ceiling for added strength. If at all possible, tunneling was conducted in stable soil not requiring shoring. The depth of a tunnel could depend on the stability of soil at different depths. Where there was loose soil the tunnel might be lined with bamboo mats and poles. Planks and timbers were used for shoring when necessary. Even brickwork was occasionally used for reinforcement. Near the surface vegetation roots helped reinforce the material overhead.

Air vents (*lo thong noi*) were made from 2–4in. hollow bamboo and pipes. They were roughly 30ft. apart, but because of angular turns and traps they might be placed at closer intervals. The more

A Special Forces NCO and MIKE Force strikers enter one of the many cave systems honeycombing Nui Coto Mountain, which rises up from the Mekong Delta. The granite mountain saw a brutal battle as the IV Corps MIKE Force cleared it. 106mm recoilless rifles were used to suppress cave entrances as flamethrower and demolition teams closed in to target the openings.

A hypothetical VC tunnel complex

This hypothetical two-level tunnel complex shows the many characteristics and features found in tunnel systems. Not all tunnel systems possessed all of these features though. All entrances and air vents would be well concealed.

1 Vertical shaft entrance. 2 Angled shaft entrance with steps. 3 Underwater entrance.
4 Air vent. 5 Family bomb shelter. 6 Air lock. 7 Water lock. 8 Water sump. 9 Punji stake trap.
10 Blast tunnel. 11 False dead-end tunnel. 12 Concealed trapdoor. 13 Storeroom.
14 Command post. 15 Personnel quarters. 16 Cadre shelter ("tepee-shelter"). 17 Latrine.
18 Kitchen with Dien Bien Phu stove. 19 Water well. 20 Niche. 21 Observation/fighting bunker in termite hill. 22 Fighting bunker. 23 Covered trench.

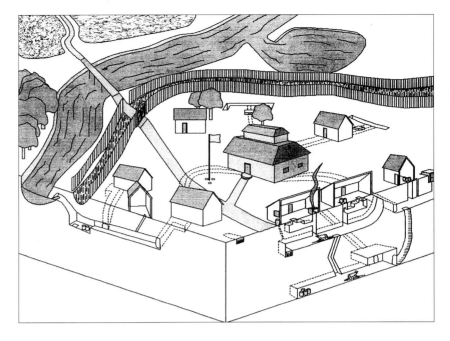

A diagram of a two-level village tunnel system, connecting most of the structures as well as defensive trenches. A small family bomb shelter is located beneath each house and connected to the tunnels; these were normally separate, though. The village is surrounded by a punji-stake-filled moat with a sharpened bamboo fence on either side. (Courtesy of Bruce Hanesalo, from *Tunnel Warfare*, Vol. 4)

turns, different levels, traps, and rooms there were, the more restricted was the air flow. There was no forced ventilation, and even with vents connected to lower levels there was little air. Vents were sometimes angled to prevent rain from entering. This would also make it difficult for above-ground searchers to determine a tunnel's route. They might also face to the east to catch the morning sun to allow warm air to enter: tunnels were cool and even cold, aggravated by the dampness. They might also face prevailing winds to provide better air circulation. Air vents emerged a couple of inches out of the ground to keep rain runoff out. They were concealed in brush, grass, inside bamboo thickets, among tree roots, in rock piles, or disguised as support poles on village structures.

Great care was taken to conceal entrances (*cua ham*). First they had to be on slightly elevated ground to prevent rainwater from pooling. They were kept as small as practical, as little as 14in. × 18in., but might be 2ft. × 2ft. and could be much larger (3ft. × 5ft.) to allow bulk supplies and equipment to enter. The trapdoors could be square, rectangular, or circular. The entry was typically framed with boards to provide a lower lip on which the trapdoor rested, or the frame was beveled allowing the trapdoor to nest into it. In both cases the trapdoor was flush with the ground. Usually the doors could be lifted completely out, but hinged doors were sometimes used. The doors had integrated camouflage and were difficult to locate. The beveled-type door was a "tray" with its sides angled inward to the bottom. It might be filled with concrete, clay, or packed earth. Layers of waterproofing plastic might be included. Small bushes or grass could be planted in the earth-filled door. Earth-filled doors had the advantage of being difficult to detect by probing unless the frame was struck. Rubber tree sap might cover the fill and the appropriate dirt, sand, or gravel embedded in it. Small wire loops served as lifting handles. Earthenware rice wine jars, cooking pots, or water barrels were placed over openings. Sometimes a leafy fresh-cut bush was simply pulled into a small opening hidden among brush. Deception was used by placing entrances in unlikely and inconspicuous places: the steep sides of inaccessible ravines, in the banks of streams and ponds just above or even below water level, inside livestock pens and beneath manure piles, fire-pits, religious shrines, deep inside brush and bamboo clumps, and even in latrines. Those inside houses were

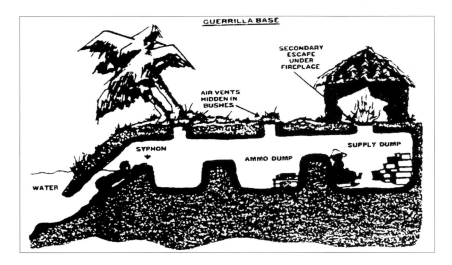

GUERRILLA BASE

SECONDARY ESCAPE UNDER FIREPLACE

AIR VENTS HIDDEN IN BUSHES

SYPHON

WATER

AMMO DUMP

SUPPLY DUMP

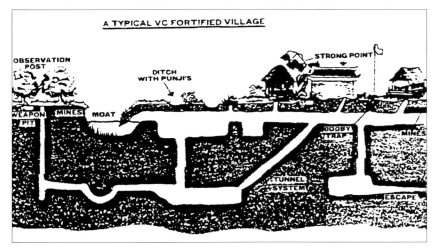

A TYPICAL VC FORTIFIED VILLAGE

OBSERVATION POST

DITCH WITH PUNJI'S

STRONG POINT

WEAPON PIT

MINES

MOAT

BOOBY TRAP

MINES

TUNNEL SYSTEM

ESCAPE

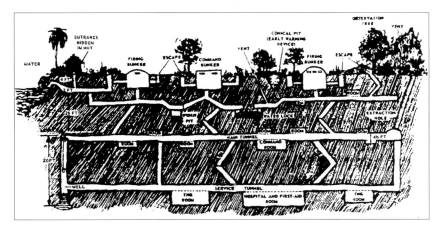

Three examples of VC tunnel systems ranging from the extremely simple (top) to an elaborate three-level system (bottom). These simplistic, two-dimensional illustrations were typical of those found in US military manuals.

concealed by sleeping mats, baskets, earthenware jars, and woodpiles. Often civilians were relied on to seal and camouflage the entry. Most entries were vertical shafts, but some sloped and might have steps cut into the earth, or log steps. Vertical shafts might have ladders, notched logs, and toe- and footholds cut in the sides, often aided by a knotted rope.

41

There were various active and passive internal defense means available. The entries might be booby-trapped, inside or out. Concealed hand grenades or Claymore mines might be command-detonated by an individual inside the tunnel, concealed in a covering position, or observing from another nearby entrance. There could be two to four entrances serving the same tunnel within 40–50m of each other. In the early days the mistake was made to place entrances too close together, making it easier for them to be detected. Dead-end tunnels were sometimes used to frustrate and confuse enemy explorers. False walls hid further tunnel sections, and concealed trapdoors hid access to lower levels. Internal trapdoors could be blocked by sandbags to halt both explorers and blast concussion. Some tunnel sections might be blocked off by up to 4ft. of earth with these escape routes known only to cadre personnel. Deadfall traps triggered by tripwires might be used along with concealed punji stake pits. Entry shafts might have false bottoms continuing down as much as 20ft. and were water-filled or bristling with punji stakes. A waiting fighter could toss a grenade into a U-shaped trap when an enemy soldier entered – with the fighter protected by the four 90-degree turns. Another might wait at a tunnel turn with a spear (as gunfire was deafening in such confined space). There are stories of poisonous snakes being hung in tunnels, and while this may have occurred, the logistics, care, and storage of the snakes, the time necessary to "install" them, and the fact that the intruders had flashlights, make it appear an impractical option.

Within a village there might be a central tunnel with numerous branches accessing different areas as well as tunnels leading out, often to a stream, river, canal, or extremely dense area of vegetation. Besides escape tunnels, those running to bodies of water provided the water supply. Tunnels could run in any imaginable pattern. Some branch tunnels were connected to bunkers. Most systems were of one level, but multi-level tunnels, up to three or even four, were found in more elaborate systems. Levels were designated by Roman numbers (*Tang* I, II, III). Many tunnel systems were simple designs, comprising a main tunnel with a few branches in which fighters and/or civilians hid. Others could be elaborate, with varying quantities of facilities depending on their use, the units using it, the numbers of personnel it would hide, and the support infrastructure. Facilities would be housed in chambers of the necessary size, through dug only as large as necessary, off the main tunnel or in branch tunnels; they might include troop quarters with hammocks or bamboo platform beds, command posts, signal centers, printing shops, briefing and class rooms, aid stations, complete hospitals and operating rooms, weapons repair shops, armories, booby trap and expedient weapons factories, storage rooms for ammunition, rations, and supplies. Rooms typically had heightened ceilings; those created in shallow tunnels were simply excavated from the surface, roofed over, backfilled, and the surface returned to its original appearance. Tiny man-sized prone dugouts were dug into the sides of tunnels for sleeping, leaving the main tunnel clear. Cone-shaped holes were dug off branch tunnels as bomb shelters. Referred to as "tepee" or "cadre" shelters, they were lined with bamboo poles. Housing several men, they were more resistant to nearby bomb blasts. The more important the facility the deeper it was, unless flood-prone. Troop quarters would be in the uppermost level to ease digging out if collapsed. Kitchens too were in the upper level to accommodate Dien Bien Phu stoves. Deep vertical shafts might serve as water wells. Water was also stocked in drums and earthenware jars.

Besides tunnels, natural caves were used in the mountains. Their size varied greatly and because they were often found in granite, they could seldom be expanded or connected.

Tackling the tunnels and fortifications

The 77-day siege of the Marine base at Khe Sanh[5] in early 1968 saw extensive NVA use of fortifications. This action took place in the extreme northwest of the RVN among forested rolling hills, gorges, and plateaux. The NVA plan was to pin down large numbers of American forces, preventing their use elsewhere during the Tet Offensive. Instead, three NVA divisions and thousands of support troops were held in place by 6,680 US troops. Khe Sanh is often thought of as an American base heavily punished by NVA barrages, but in reality the base and its hill outposts received only 11,100 rounds of artillery and rockets. The US shot back 159,000 rounds of artillery and dropped almost as much bomb tonnage (114,810 tons) around Khe Sanh in three months as B-29s rained on Japan in 1945. The NVA lost an estimated 10–15,000 men while the defenders lost some 300.

While the NVA no doubt would have attempted to storm the base if the opportunity presented itself, they made little real effort to do so, other than giving the appearance that carrying the base was the goal. Attack trenches, mortar and AA positions, fighting/living bunkers, base camps, limestone caves, and supply caches honeycombed the hills around the base.

The hills, ridges, and gorges around Khe Sanh were saturated by fighter-bombers and B-52 "Arc Light" strikes. Thirty-five B-52 sorties delivered over 1,000 tons of bombs every 24 hours, with cells of three bombers arriving every one to three hours. Between nine and 12 "Mini-" and "Micro-Arc Lights" were delivered nightly consisting of up to two hundred and sixty 4.2in., 105mm, 155mm and 175mm rounds plus fifty-six 500 lb. bombs into small areas. The targets were detected by ground and aerial observation, patrols, and various sensors. The NVA at Khe Sanh employed kilometers of winding assault trenches, sneaking toward the base mainly from the east and southeast. At the head of these 3ft.-wide, 4ft.-deep trenches were T-shaped trenches perpendicular to the base's perimeter. Short slit trenches thrust out a few feet forward of these trenches with 4ft.-diameter personnel pits at the head of each. It was from these trenches that the sappers and infantrymen would charge the base; however, only a few small-scale attacks were actually launched.

After the siege was lifted patrols investigated former enemy-held areas to study the effects of this massive firepower. While the NVA had suffered extensive casualties, the amount of ordnance required was massive. There were numerous instances when troop units were caught in the open while moving, with some units ceasing to exist. The bomb damage inflicted on the fortifications, though, was surprisingly light. Hits from 750 lb. and 1,000 lb. bombs, with their crater lips only 6–10ft. from bunkers, left them intact. Walls and roofs did not even collapse. There were few indications that concussion killed or seriously disabled occupants. No dead were found inside, but corpses were discovered on the surface having been killed by fragments. Presumably, if these bodies had not been taken away then others would not have been removed from bunkers. Fighter-bombers aiming at the center of mass of multiple positions often had a marginal effect. One example is a triangular 12.7mm AA machine gun position. A 750 lb. or 1,000 lb. bomb landed directly in between the three pits, creating a 20ft.-diameter, 10ft.-deep crater; the pits were 36–60ft. apart and remained unscathed. There were 2–3-man fighting/living bunkers within 10ft. of 38ft.-diameter, 18ft.-deep craters – and the bunkers still survived. Scores of fighting

Mity Mite blower

The "Mity Mite" was a man-portable commercial pesticide blower; thousands were purchased by the Army, and it was officially known as the M106 riot control agent disperser-fogger. It weighed 25 lb. without fuel and CS powder and was powered by a two-cycle gasoline engine. It held 1qt. of gasoline-oil fuel sufficient to run it for half an hour. The tank held 10 lb. of CS or 3 gal of liquid pesticide; they were also used to spray for mosquitoes and flies. A 2ft.-long flexible tube and nozzle was fitted. Operators were provided two hours' training and were required to wear protective masks. When needed, the blowers, fuel, and CS containers were helicoptered in. Tunnel entrances were covered with ponchos, the edges sealed with dirt, the nozzle inserted in the poncho's hood opening, and the opening was sealed with tape. Another method was to place the top half of a 5-gal can into the entrance. A hole was cut in the top, the nozzle inserted, and sealed with tape. Other known openings were sealed by shoveling earth over entrances or plugging air vents with mud or vegetation. Mity Mites were also used to flush out smoke from tunnels and to blow fresh air in to aid tunnel rats.

---

[5] See Osprey Campaign 150, *Khe Sanh 1967–68.*

A tunnel rat fitted with the less than successful cap-mounted lamp, voice-activated telephone communications system, and a Smith & Wesson .38-cal Special revolver with silencer and aiming light.

and living bunkers on NVA-occupied hills were examined. Hilltops and sides were pocked by hundreds of artillery and bomb craters and much of the vegetation was burned off by napalm. However, unless a bunker took a direct hit, most remained undamaged.

The general conclusions concerning the effects of artillery and air strikes were summarized in the study as follows:

- NVA bunkers withstood anything but a direct hit by artillery or bombs.
- Delay fuzing produced the best effects against bunkers; however, much of the ordnance penetrated too deep before detonating in the soft soil.
- Super-quick fuzing was effective for stripping away camouflage to expose positions, but was not effective against bunkers.
- Napalm was not effective for burning off large areas of foliage. WP artillery rounds were more effective.
- 105mm and 155mm howitzers were not effective against bunkers.

In addition to artillery and bombs, direct attack munitions were employed against bunkers and tunnels. Mortars had little effect unless delayed fuzing was used. The 60mm would simply bounce off the target, as it lacked the weight to penetrate even light bunker roofs. The 81mm and 4.2in. mortars fared better, but a direct hit was necessary with a delayed fuze. Mortars were useful, like artillery, for blowing away camouflage to allow bunkers to be attacked directly. Infantry units had very few explosive-firing heavy weapons because of the difficulty of man-packing them and their ammunition over rough terrain in a sweltering climate. M72 and M72A1 light antitank weapons (LAW – 66mm single-shot disposable rocket launcher) were used, but required a close-range hit directly on a firing port to be effective. The effects inside a bunker were often disappointing. The 40mm M79 grenade launcher too required a round to be placed in the port, a difficult task owing to its small size. The Marines sometimes used the 3.5in. M20A1B1 bazooka, but it was little more effective than the LAW, which weighed less than a 3.5in. rocket. 90mm M67 and jeep-mounted 106mm M40A1 recoilless rifles were seldom available, as were man-packed flamethrowers. Vehicle-mounted flamethrowers were sometimes employed and while effective against bunkers and for burning off concealing vegetation, they had little effect on tunnel entrances. The fireball simply did not travel down vertical shafts and enter the main tunnel for any distance.

Often it took soldiers executing a direct assault backed by covering fire, not only on the targeted bunker but to suppress adjacent positions, to reduce a bunker. Hand grenades and C4 satchel charges usually did the job, but there might be small hide holes inside or escape tunnels/covered trenches. Hand grenade types included fragmentation, demolition (concussion), WP, and CS. Claymore mines were pushed into ports, the soldier rolling to one side as another detonated it via its 100ft. electric firing wire. Bangalore torpedoes were thrust through ports and detonated with shattering effect.

Clues indicating the presence of tunnels included slight depressions in or around bamboo thickets, worn places on bamboo the enemy had used as handholds, urine tracks in vegetated areas away from trails, faint trails that ended at foliage clumps, the smell or presence of fresh-cooked food found in huts with no one nearby, a lone female or pre-teenager with no one else nearby who may have closed and camouflaged tunnel entrances, and the smell of food or body odor in bamboo and brush clumps indicating air vents. An essential Vietnamese condiment was Nuc-Mam, a strong-smelling, fermented fish sauce. Once the extent of the tunnel systems was realized, when apparently abandoned villages were found the search for tunnels began immediately. Scout and tracker dogs as well as "people-sniffers"[6] were used to detect enemy bases.

Once a tunnel entrance was discovered, all-round security was established and the immediate area checked for booby traps. Nearby clumps of foliage were searched for covering snipers and other entrances. The trapdoor was removed by grappling hooks or blown in with demolitions. Additional demolition charges were lowered into the shaft and detonated to blast away tripwires, mechanical booby traps and punji stakes, and kill or drive away occupants. M18 colored or AN-M8 white smoke grenades or 12 lb. M1A1 white smoke pots were dropped in, and the surrounding area observed for smoke emitting from vents. This did not always work, as airflow was poor, or the drifting smoke might be halted by U-shaped water and air traps, which also halted CS. Once the general pattern was known "Mity Mite" blowers would blow in air to clear the smoke for tunnel rats to enter. Other discovered entrances were opened to aid venting, demolition charges detonated, and the openings covered by riflemen. Sometimes a Huey helicopter was landed with an air compressor and a 50ft. or 100ft. hose was run into a tunnel entrance or vent to pump in air for tunnel rats.

C4 satchel charges are lowered to a tunnel rat for the destruction of key areas inside the tunnel. The camouflage has been cleared away.

Tunnel rats

When the extent of the tunnels began to be realized in early 1966 volunteer infantrymen and engineers began exploring tunnel systems to rout out the enemy and recover hidden weapons and supplies. The ARVN, fully aware of the tunnels, had avoided any thought of entering them. The presence of the tunnels was known, but the role they played and how much impact they had on the overall tactical situation was not understood. In 1963, ARVN officers discussed means of combating tunnels, but there were no real recommendations on how to do this. ARVN soldiers are said to have failed to report tunnels and even concealed exposed entrances for fear of being sent in.

Early arriving American units had heard of the tunnels, but their extent and value to the enemy was not understood. Units conducting search and destroy operations in VC strongholds such as the Iron Triangle and Ho Bo Woods were mystified by the little enemy activity they found. This resulted in a false sense of success during these operations. The initial US policy was to "destroy" the tunnels by blowing in known entrances as was done with Japanese tunnels and caves in World War II. Because of the unknown extent of the tunnels and the many undiscovered entrances, this effort was futile. The first tentative tunnel

---

[6] The helicopter-mounted XM2 (E63) or XM3 airborne olfactonic personnel detector or "people-sniffer" detected the enemy by sensing chemicals in the air given off by human activity, including perspiration, urine, campfire smoke, and engine exhaust. It was ineffective if there were civilians in the area.

A group of infantrymen pull a tunnel rat from an entrance, no doubt with a sense of urgency. Behind them appears to be a spoil pile, which the VC have failed to cart away, probably leading to the tunnel's discovery.

explorations also discovered documents of intelligence value and weapon and supply stocks. It was deemed necessary to recover or destroy these.

The first known American to venture into a tunnel was Platoon Sergeant Stewart Green of the 25th Infantry Division. On January 11, 1966 he hesitantly entered a tunnel in the Cu Chi area in an unsuccessful effort to convince VC to surrender. Soon after Captain Herbert Thorton of the 25th Infantry Division's 9th Chemical Detachment was tasked with developing methods to search and neutralize tunnels.

Tunnel neutralization was an attempt to cause VC casualties near the entrances, collapse tunnels, and make at least a portion of the tunnels uninhabitable in the short term. Tear gas grenades were one means to achieve this. A more effective method was the Mity Mite blower. Dispersed CS and smoke grenades displaced oxygen and could cause suffocation in confined enclosures.

Untrained soldiers volunteered to tentatively explore tunnels in the early days. They went in with only jungle fatigue trousers, an undershirt, cigarette filters as ear plugs, and carrying a .45-cal M1911A1 pistol and flashlight. They seldom penetrated far. It was soon realized that specially trained and equipped volunteers were necessary. "Tunnel rats," originally called "tunnel runners," were infantrymen, engineers, and chemical troops. The Army, of course, attempted to formalize them as "tunnel exploration personnel." The Australians originally called them "tunnel ferrets."

Tunnel rat volunteers were small, wiry men,[7] of basically the same stature as their quarry. Claustrophobia and fear of darkness would preclude any sufferers from attempting this job. The volunteers also had to possess a great deal of courage to penetrate into a maze of tight tunnels of unknown layout and content – a pitch black, foul-smelling environment filled with perils, what they called the "black echo." There was a high probability of booby traps, waiting VC, poor air, and all sorts of vermin and critters. They did this job willingly, collecting a great deal of respect. Many had a hunter's mentality: they would go after their quarry with a vengeance. Divisions set up schools to train tunnel rats in tunnel layout, defenses, booby traps, search techniques, tunnel mapping, communications, use of CS and demolitions, and the like. They had

---

[7] An episode of *Tour of Duty*, a 1987–90 Vietnam combat TV series, depicted midgets being employed as tunnel rats. This is completely false. The Army minimum male height was 5ft.

to be able to quickly change flashlight batteries and bulbs and reload and clear weapons by feel. Engineers brought their demolitions expertise to this role, and chemical troops operated the blowers and assembled the CS devices. They operated in 4 to 6 "tunnel exploitation and denial teams". The tunnel rats' attitude was exemplified by their unofficial motto: *Non Gratum Anus Rodentum* – "Not Worth a Rat's Ass"!

Once other entrances and vents had been located by seeping smoke and detailed searches, the selected entrance had been blasted open, and the smoke had been vented out by blowers, one to three tunnel rats entered. The lead man would usually have a rope tied to his ankle or around his waist to pull him out if killed or wounded. No tunnel rat was left behind. They seldom ventured more than a couple of hundred feet. Those going further would untie their rope. The exploration team would measure the length of tunnel sections and report direction changes by compass bearing and rooms, entry shafts and air vents to a team on the surface via telephone. The surface team would follow along uncovering entrances and vents.

The camouflage and trapdoor having been removed, a tunnel rat examines the entry shaft for booby traps before descending. He carries the two most important items of equipment for a tunnel rat: a Colt .45-cal M1911A1 pistol and a TL-122D flashlight.

The Army's various infantry training centers constructed replica Vietnamese defended villages and some of these boasted tunnel systems. These were rather simplistic, usually a tunnel running across the village with one or two branches and an entry at the ends, possibly one or two set in its length. They were constructed of 4ft.-diameter corrugated steel pipe, making it impossible to practice plotting routes with magnetic compasses. The author's experience in the tunnels of Ft. Polk, Louisiana was limited, owing to them being flooded by the high water table.

They explored the tunnels to at least gain some idea of their extent. While large systems were not explored entirely because of the time and danger, it provided an indication that there were other entrances throughout an area. As these were discovered other sections of a system would be partly explored. Intelligence documents, equipment, and supplies would be recovered, and whether the tunnel was indeed occupied was determined. Occasionally occupants were coached out by Kit Carson Scouts.[8]

Teams assembled kits with two each of the following items: 100ft. of rope, body armor vests, grappling hooks, M9 or M17 gas masks, TA-1/PT sound-powered telephones, pairs of work gloves, pairs of knee pads, and pairs of earplugs plus six 6-volt flashlights and a one-mile spool of field telephone wire. Another kit example contained two each of the following: compasses, 12-volt flashlights, Hi Standard .22-cal HD automatic pistols sometimes with silencers, M7 bayonets, 12in. and 36in. probing rods, four M18 smoke grenades, 12 CS grenades, four cans of insect repellent, an entrenching tool, a TA-1/PT phone and a half-mile wire spool. The AN/PAS-6 metascope, an infrared flashlight and viewer, saw some use. Starlight scopes could not be used as they intensified ambient light (star and moonlight, sky-glow) and these were not present within tunnels. Body armor was seldom worn as it was too restricting. Even gloves and kneepads were dispensed with by some for being too restricting. The Army issued only six purpose-built tunnel exploration kits in 1966. With each

[8] These were defected VC who were validated and accepted as *Hoi Chanhs* (ralliers) under the Chieu Hoi (open arms) Program implemented by the RVN Government in 1963. They were attached to US units and were invaluable as scouts, for locating booby traps and tunnels, communicating with civilians, and the like.

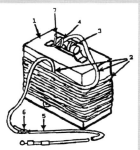

The bunker bomb was an incendiary satchel charge. A metal ammunition box was filled three-quarters full of gasoline and motor oil (1-gal) and the lid taped shut (1). Some 50ft. of detonating cord was wrapped in 15 horizontal turns around the box leaving two 2ft.-long free ends (2). An AN-M14 incendiary or M34 WP grenade or M49A1 trip flare was taped to the carrying handle (3). One free end of the detcord was taped under the grenade/trip flare safety lever and the lever taped down (7). A non-electric blasting cap (6) with a 6–10-second delay fuze was taped to the other free end of the detcord with a fuze igniter (5). When ready the grenade/trip flare safety pin was pulled (the lever being held in place as it was taped to the body). The fuze igniter was pulled and the bomb thrown into a bunker firing port or tunnel entrance. The detcord imploded the box, blew off the grenade/trip flare safety lever, and the fuel exploded. The approximately 0.33 lb. of PETN contained in the 50ft. of detcord was equivalent to about 0.5 lb. of TNT and created considerable fragmentation. The blast and flash radius was at least 5m, and fragmentation somewhat further. There were numerous versions of this expedient weapon.

The AN/PAS-6 metascope was a two-piece assemblage with a flashlight-like infrared light source (upper component) and a 1x infrared viewer. It was compact, measuring 4.5in. × 4.5in. × 6in., and was sometimes used by tunnel rats.

came a Smith & Wesson .38-cal Special revolver with a silencer and aiming light. The aiming light was unnecessary and the silencer too long, making the revolver unbalanced. A miner's light with a bite-switch was fitted onto a baseball cap. The cap's visor blocked the light beam and the switch malfunctioned. A bone-conduction microphone was fitted requiring a wire reel slung on the back. An improved tunnel kit was requested in 1967, but the 250 kits were not issued until June 1968. Seventy-five S&W .44-cal Magnum Model 29 revolvers were modified and issued in 1969 as tunnel weapons; they were inexplicably withdrawn after six months' use. They had no sight, a 3in. smoothbore barrel, and fired a round loaded with 15 lead shots. A knife was essential, the most common being the M3 and Kay-Bar Mk 2 fighting knifes, M7 bayonet, and Air Force survival knife. Hand grenades were not carried. Limited use was made of shotguns, but even with sawn-off barrels they were too cumbersome.

Tunnel rats experienced close-quarter shootouts, hand-to-hand fights, booby traps, lingering tear gas and smoke, insufficient oxygen, flooded tunnels and traps, and cave-ins. Issue gas masks protected them from CS and inhaling smoke, but offered no protection from carbon monoxide or the lack of oxygen displaced by CS and smoke. The first Australian ferret to die was Corporal Bob Bowtell of the Australian Royal Engineers. After forcing his way through an internal trapdoor he became stuck, and despite the best efforts of his comrades asphyxiated in the smoke-filled tunnel. A great deal of caution had to be used when emerging from a tunnel from an opening other than the one used to enter the tunnel, for fear of being shot by friendlies. Regardless of the inherent dangers, tunnel rat casualties were surprisingly light.

Destroying the tunnels

Tunnels were destroyed as far as possible by blowing in the entrance shafts. Tunnel collapse required 37.5 lb. crates of C4 or 40 lb. ammonium nitrate cratering charges emplaced at junctions, in rooms, near entrances, and at intervals in long tunnels. A little-used method to collapse tunnels within 7ft. of the surface was to helicopter in compressed acetylene gas cylinders. A hose was inserted in a sealed tunnel opening and the gas valve opened. It would require several cylinders as each held only 325 cubic ft. Air and water locks as well as sandbagged internal trapdoors blocked the spread of CS and acetylene. When detonated by explosive charges acetylene flash-burned at over 5,000°F. A combination of explosive charges and acetylene proved effective on tunnels as deep as 20ft. Tanks and dozers were used to collapse shallow tunnels, no more

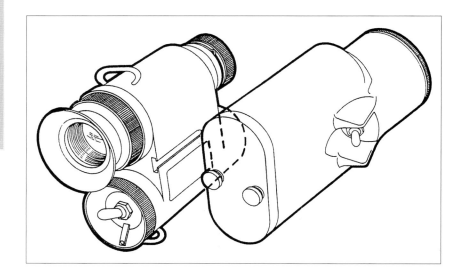

than 3ft. deep. This was difficult as the track had to follow the twisting tunnel's course and could become stuck after the collapse. It was very rare in multiple-level systems for those deeper than the first level to be destroyed by any means.

In January 1967 during Operation *Cedar Falls* the 1st Infantry Division, acting on information provided by a captured VC, swept an area 6km south of Rach Bap. As base camps, caches, and bunker complexes were discovered so were tunnel entrances and vents. It was realized that a huge tunnel system snaked through the area. Hundreds of meters were explored and a great deal of documents of intelligence value and supplies and weapons were recovered. Almost 10,000m of tunnels, four fortified villages, 27 base camps, and 60 scattered bunkers were destroyed. The VC stronghold at Ben Suc was leveled by bulldozers collapsing tunnels and crushing bunkers. In a further effort to destroy tunnels honeycombing the area a large pit was bulldozed in the village center, filled with 10,000 lb. of explosives (much of which had deteriorated and could not safely be used for normal demolition tasks), and detonated. It is not known how effective this was.

As is often mentioned, the concealment of moving troops, base camps, caches, and defensive positions provided by natural vegetation was a major factor in VC/NVA tactics. Caterpillar D7E and D9 bulldozers fitted with special tree-felling plows were employed to clear land along highways and around bases to deny the enemy cover, and to destroy fortifications. Additionally, herbicides were used extensively. Over 8,100,000-gal of defoliants were sprayed by the US Air Force. This does not include that sprayed by the Army and RVN from the air and on the ground. Agent Orange and other herbicides killed off the vegetation around vast base areas, along trail networks, around Free World Bases, and wide swathes of terrain to allow movement to be detected. The vegetation would die soon after application, but in some cases, depending on the type of vegetation, its density, and local soil and seasonal conditions it still provided a degree of concealment. The plants are hardy and in the tropics they often grew back quickly.

The legality of CS

CS is a non-lethal riot control agent and its use is legal under international law. In 1965 an American reporter described the use of CS by ARVN troops as equating to toxic chemical warfare; its use was prohibited by US forces at the time. In September a Marine unit employed CS to flush out VC entrenched in a tunnel and bunker system; reports indicated large numbers of civilians including women and children were among them. CS was used to clear the complex and 400 civilians were recovered without injury. Regardless, two days later all commanders were reminded that CS was prohibited. Because of the successful employment of CS in this instance its use was authorized later in the month in the Iron Triangle. On November 3, 1965 the Joint Chiefs of Staff approved the general use of CS and CN (an earlier tear gas). CS was widely used throughout the war to clear tunnels and fortifications, by patrols to break contact with the enemy, and was spread to deny the enemy access to specific areas. While contentious, its use saved lives on both sides; the alternatives were high explosives, WP, and flame weapons. The VC/NVA referred to it as "toxic gas," but occasionally used it themselves.

A Navy SEAL secures detonating cord to a 1.25 lb. M112 C4 demolition charge while preparing to blow in the entrance to a VC bunker in the Mekong Delta. The bunker is mostly below ground with an earth and log roof. (US Navy)

The test of battle

The small bunker was the most common fighting position and shelter employed by the VC/NVA. They were small, crowded, smelly, and dirty. They could be dusty, damp, or partly flooded depending on the season. Even with a waterproofing layer incorporated into the overhead cover they still took in water during heavy rains. Because they were below ground with a thick earth and log covering they were pleasantly cool in the oppressive heat, and further protected from the sun by the requisite overhead foliage. Fighters slept on the ground cushioned by leaves and fronds or in jammed-together hammocks. Once completed they soon became a haven for pests and vermin. Bunkers and other positions which had not been occupied had to be entered with caution and the unwanted residents turned out.

RIGHT A US soldier uses a large earthenware pot for bathing. Such jars, found in a variety of sizes, were used for water and food storage inside tunnels. They were also buried flush with the ground in underground rooms for use as latrines.

OPPOSITE The Cu Chi tunnels and the Iron Triangle.

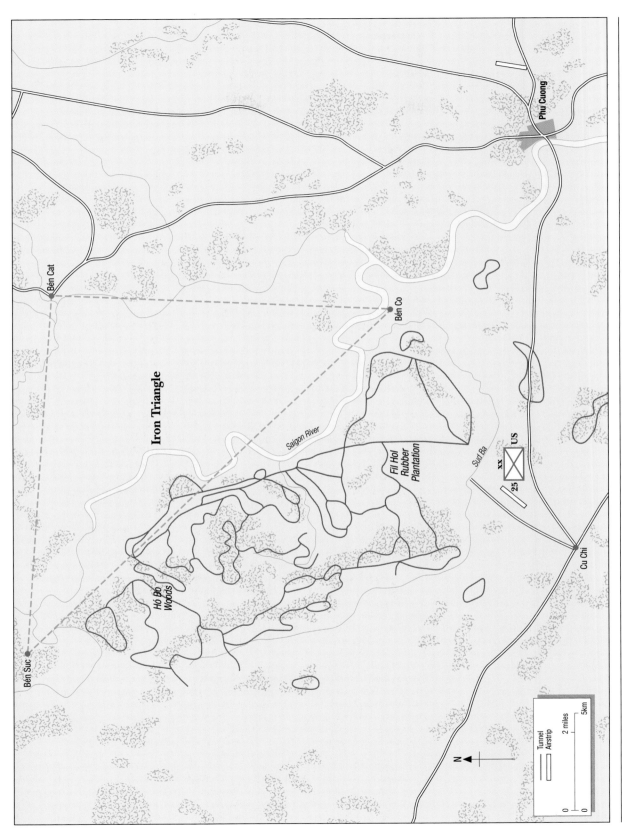

Iron Triangle

Bén Súc

Bén Cat

Bén Co

Hó Bó
Woods

Saigon River

Fil Hol
Rubber
Plantation

Suoi Ba

Phu Cuong

Cu Chi

xx
25   US

N

Tunnel
Airstrip

0   2 miles
0   5km

51

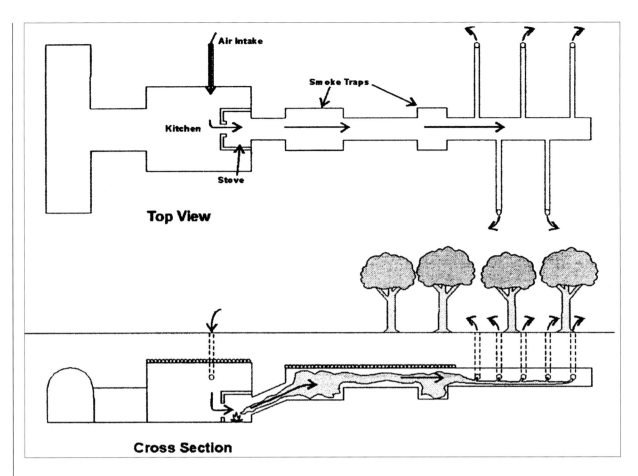

Top View

Air Intake

Smoke Traps

Kitchen

Stove

Cross Section

A plan view and cross-section of a below-ground Dien Bien Phu stove. These had to be located near the surface, dug from ground level, and then covered over. They did not work well, and the kitchen was often filled with smoke.

As fighting positions, the bunkers performed in a satisfactory manner. Because of positioning, usually excellent camouflage, and low profile they were difficult to detect. This allowed the defenders to engage approaching Free World forces when desired, that is, at close range and from a favorable direction. They were difficult to hit with fire for the same reasons. The small firing ports and entrances enhanced this aspect. Because of the limited number and small size of the near ground-level firing ports, the defenders had to have a high degree of confidence in their neighboring positions. They in turn were expected to provide effective, mutually supporting fire for their neighbors.

Artillery, helicopter rockets, mortars, and bombs required a direct or an immediately adjacent hit to destroy a bunker. A heavy bomb or shell might partly or fully collapse a bunker, but this was rare. Survivors frequently dug themselves out, sometimes with the aid of other unit members. Napalm bombs had only limited effect on bunkers. Since they were usually beneath trees, bamboo, or brush, the bombs ignited when they struck the vegetation. The fireballs, while impressive, immediately bellowed upward, and dissipated. Troops in the open were killed, but those in bunkers often survived. However, the jellied fuel might enter ports and entrances and oxygen could be consumed to suffocate occupants. The author witnessed areas of thick, high bamboo and brush with the upper layers burned, but the lower half still green and untouched. A prolonged heavy artillery or aerial bombardment was an ordeal, though, regardless of how well constructed a bunker was.

If attackers were able to gain an advantageous position or destroyed supporting bunkers, the bunker could become a death trap. It was difficult if not impossible to determine what the fate of adjacent positions was, and when attackers had flanked the bunker. There was no defense against grenades and satchel charges once attackers had gained a blind spot. Withdrawing from a bunker could be an extremely hazardous undertaking. One might exit into a hale of fire. Escape tunnels and trenches were not always available. To stay meant either surrender, or being blown apart or incinerated with the inglorious fate of the bunker being filled in, becoming one's grave.

On one occasion the author sought cover in a 141st NVA Infantry bunker as described previously. While the bunker received nothing like what American forces would blast it with, both 82mm mortar and RPG-2 rounds struck it. Earth fell through gaps in the log overhead cover and it was dusty, but secure. Used to fighting in the relative "openness" of the jungle, the restricted field of vision through the small firing port was disconcerting with no vision to the flanks and rear. This took getting used to.

Open-topped fighting positions such as trenches and foxholes had limited value and the occupants stood little chance of surviving. The VC/NVA habitually dug niches into foxholes if more substantial overhead cover was not available. They had to expose heads and shoulders to small-arms fire, high-explosive and WP airburst artillery,[9] artillery and aerial-delivered cluster munitions, helicopter flechette rockets, and mortars – which all made fast work of reducing these positions. These were also vulnerable to hand and 40mm grenades.

Life underground

Life within a tunnel was far from cushy. The constricting tunnels, cramped spaces, crowding, perpetual blackness, poor air, carbon monoxide, and fear of discovery and attack were a way of life. It is said that inhabitants remained underground for years, but this is mostly an exaggeration. There were people who did spend prolonged periods underground though. In areas under intense pressure that experienced frequent Free World sweeps, they were indeed fearful of creeping out, even at night. Footprints, a dropped cartridge, or spilt grains of rice may not have been noticed by those venturing out, but could be discovered by the enemy in daylight.

Rarely, and in critical facilities only, hand- or foot-pedal-powered or battery-operated electric lights were provided. Candles, kerosene and oil lamps, and flashlights were the most common light sources. Nut-oil lamps were made of larger cartridge casings with their mouth crimped shut and a wick inserted. Often the inhabitants endured long periods of darkness, and claustrophobia and fear of the dark were debilitating to some.

Cave-ins, flooding, and depleted oxygen were natural hazards. Work in cramped conditions was unending to expand and repair the tunnels and maintain the stowed supplies and equipment as well as their own gear. Any communicable diseases spread rapidly in such close quarters and the cool, damp environment aggravated illnesses. It did not take long for co-habitation of the tunnels to occur. Spiders, centipedes, scorpions, mosquitoes, fleas, roaches, ants, snakes, rats, mice, and bats would quickly move in though air vents and trapdoors, all of which were poisonous, bit, stung, or carried serious diseases.

The Dien Bien Phu kitchens did not work very well with smoke backing up and the food being poorly cooked. The inhabitants might cook outside at night or rely on villagers to cook and deliver food then. Fresh hot meals were rare, although grilled rats were a treat. Personal hygiene was poor. Bathing was unheard of in the filthy tunnels with their crumbing ceilings and dust. Water was often in short supply. Even in tunnels with riverside exits they were fearful of leaving traces and stirring up mud if they ventured out.

Three means of disposing of human waste were available. Large earthenware jugs with lids were buried in latrine room floors. They were sealed with mud

---

[9] When WP rounds burst they showered 5,000°F (2,760°C) burning particles into open positions, which would burn through flesh and ignite flammable materials, whilst creating a white smoke screen.

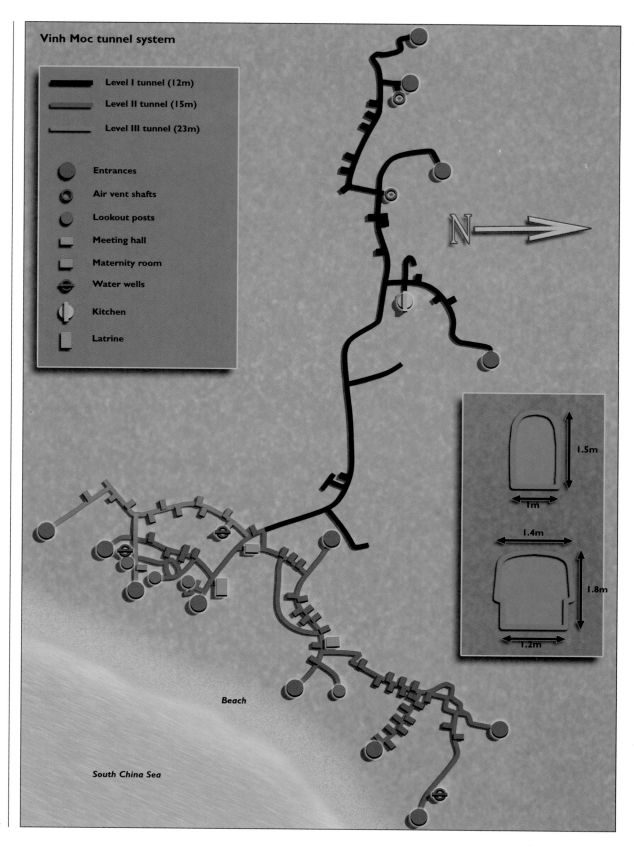

Vinh Moc tunnel system

Level I tunnel (12m)
Level II tunnel (15m)
Level III tunnel (23m)

Entrances
Air vent shafts
Lookout posts
Meeting hall
Maternity room
Water wells
Kitchen
Latrine

N

1.5m
1m
1.4m
1.8m
1.2m

Beach

South China Sea

A cross-section of the 1m-wide, 1.5m-high arched whitewashed segment of the Vinh Moc tunnels. The exit door was set in the bluff overlooking the beach. (Vietnam Tourist Bureau)

and covered once filled. Recovered Free World metal ammunition cans were airtight-sealed with latch-type lids and rubber gaskets. These cans were carelessly discarded by ground units and thrown from helicopters when empty and collected by VC sympathizers. They were used as "chamber pots" and at night emptied outside, often being picked up and returned by villagers. In an emergency when Free World forces were overhead, one might have to dig a cat-hole where one happened to be and relieve oneself. In some instances dead VC were buried in the tunnels, usually in small niches dug in tunnel sides, the body entombed in a fetal position, and sealed with clay. This was intended as a temporary measure to prevent Free World forces from determining VC casualties, but they sometimes remained. Human waste, the odors of festering wounds and sickness, the dank environment, mold, cooking smoke and food odors, weapons oil, body odor, the close smell of earth, and possibly corpses assailed the inhabitants.

When Free World forces were in the area, tunnel inhabitants remained totally silent with minimal movement, although there were instances when searchers heard voices through vents and hidden trapdoors. The wounded were held in tunnels until they could be moved for treatment; few actually possessed hospitals. Some died, some went mad. In an effort to protect themselves from

LEFT **Vinh Moc tunnel system**

The underground village of Vinh Moc in North Vietnam consisted of 1,600m of whitewashed clay tunnels (sections of which are shown in the inset illustrations) and arranged in three levels. Level III, lying roughly parallel to the beach, was some 23m below the bluffs overlooking the South China Sea and was just above sea level. The original surface village was just to the north end of Level III near the shore. The small family rooms are in the alcoves lining the main tunnels. Large quantities of rice and supplies were stored in the tunnels while awaiting shipment south.

An XM3 airborne olfactonic personnel detector, or "people-sniffer," mounted aboard a UH1H Huey helicopter. The sensor head is at the end of the tube fastened to the skid. Such high-tech equipment was only marginally effective.

CS gas, homemade gas masks were fabricated from parachute cloth and linen with charcoal filters. Sometimes they were reduced to using urine-soaked rags tied around their faces.

Cu Chi

The tunnels of Cu Chi verge on the legendary. They were undoubtedly the largest and most developed example of any tunnel system, and few others even approached Cu Chi's scale. Cu Chi is a small town in the southern portion of Cu Chi District, itself part of Binh Duong Province, an area some 25 miles northwest of Saigon. Most of the tunnels were found in the northern third of the district, an area about 4 × 12 miles. In the center of the district and south of the tunnels was Cu Chi town, the main base for the US 25th Infantry Division. Elements of the 18th ARVN Division were also based in the area.

The tunnels were begun in the early 1950s and gradually developed during the war with France. When guerrilla warfare resumed in the south in 1959 their expansion greatly increased and by the time the 25th Infantry Division arrived in March 1966 the tunnels were well developed. They were located beneath the

Fil Hol Rubber Plantation just north of the division's base and the sprawling Ho Bo Woods further north. This was an important region to the VC, bordering the southwest side of the Iron Triangle, as it contained vast farmlands of rice paddies, rubber, and orchards. It also offered key infiltration routes to Saigon from NVA base areas in Cambodia to the north and west.

The extent of the tunnels has been reported as stretching to "hundreds of miles," but in reality it is probably about 75 miles, though this by no means belittles their extent. Civilians of the area had a long tradition of resisting the Saigon government and most were loyal to the VC, which operated a "shadow government" to administer the area. Thousands of VC fighters and villagers could hide in the tunnels from which they operated and supported transient NVA units. Three VC headquarters were housed in the tunnels: the Saigon/Gia Dinh District Military Headquarters; Saigon/Gia Dinh District Political Headquarters; and Cu Chi District Military Headquarters. There were also various VC unit headquarters, such as those of the 7th Infantry, 8th Artillery (rocket), and C10 Sapper battalions.

When Free World forces entered an area their enemy would disappear into the tunnels to hide, move to other areas if the local tunnels were discovered, or move reinforcements to the threatened areas to emerge and execute hit-and-run attacks when and where they desired before disappearing underground. They were also able to conduct large-scale ambushes by moving troops into roadside attack sites, transport rockets to attack Free World bases, and reposition units in other areas without detection. Some emerged near potential helicopter landing zones. The main tunnels were a labyrinth of looping tunnels providing alternative routes to different sectors in case some were neutralized.

In some areas the tunnels boasted as many as four levels. First-level tunnels were typically 7–10ft. underground with the lowest about 30ft., but no doubt this varied from area to area. Branch tunnels ran off the main tunnels terminating in a bunker, underground room, or house. Some bunkers were hollowed-out termite mounds and hillocks with no external entrance, only a tunnel, making them even harder to detect. Many of the tunnels were simply lengthy passages for troop movement. Others held troop and family quarters, storerooms, workshops, kitchens, aid stations, hospitals, command posts, signal posts, meeting rooms, classrooms, even a cinema – the tunnels of Cu Chi were often referred to as an "underground city." The villages in the area had their own protective tunnels, which usually connected to the main tunnels.

Parts of the system were discovered, explored, and neutralized, but it was never defeated. Destroyed tunnels would be rebuilt or new ones dug. Thousands of tons of earth were removed and hidden in the process. One reason the system was so extensive was the laterite and clay soil. During the dry season it was as hard as concrete and little digging was accomplished. This was also the season in which most combat operations were conducted and it was more difficult to destroy the tunnels. During the wet season the soil became damp, but this made tunneling easy.

The first major operation that resulted in a discovery of an extended tunnel system was Operation *Crimp* conducted in January 1966 by the 25th Infantry Division and 173d Airborne Brigade with 1st Battalion, Royal Australian Regiment attached. A year later the same units, joined by the 1st Infantry Division and 11th Armored Cavalry Regiment, undertook Operation *Cedar Falls* in the same area. American and Australian tunnel rats explored thousands of meters of tunnels recovering significant equipment, supplies, and documents. While enemy casualties were high during these operations, the activities by no means came close to pacifying the area or discovered the full extent of the tunnels. In many instances civilians, when they could be found, were relocated to government-controlled areas, but even though their families were removed the VC fighters remained and continued the fight. The expansion of the tunnels continued through the war.

VC booby traps

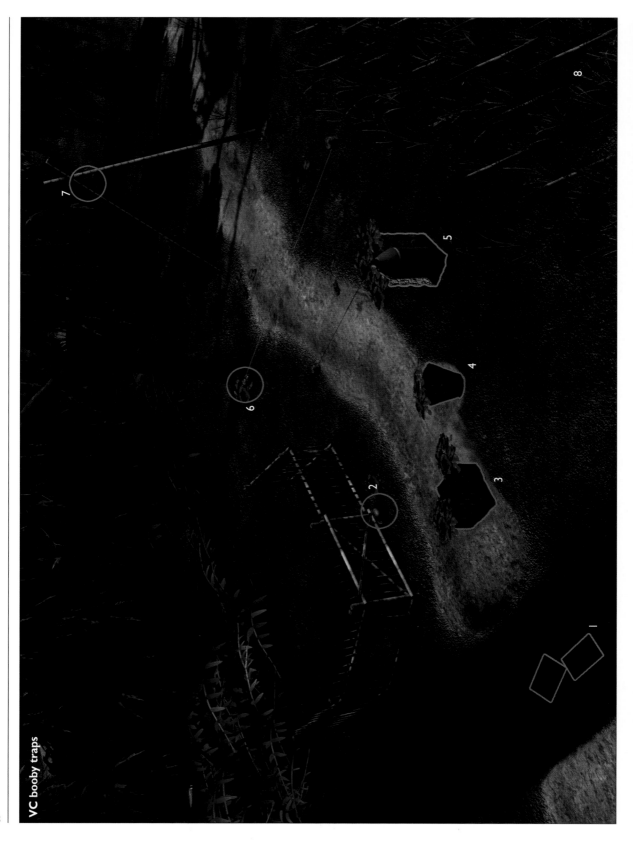

The types of booby traps, the materials and munitions they were made from, their means of activation, and methods of concealment were endless. The devices depicted here represent common examples. Extremely elaborate and complex booby traps are described in many publications, but most were very simple devices. Camouflage has been removed here for clarity: they were normally very well concealed. Such booby traps would be incorporated into the defense of base camps, villages, and other VC sites. The VC used a wide variety of signs to warn of the presence of booby traps such as stones arranged in patterns, combinations of sticks laid on the ground, notches on tree trucks, and tufts of grass tied in knots.

1 Nail boards wired to rocks on a stream bottom.
2 Hand grenade with the pin pulled and the safety lever wedged under a gate.
3 Punji stake pit, a traditional design.
4 Punji stake pit with downward angled stakes to snag the calf when withdrawn.
5 Recovered dud artillery projectile with tripwire-activated fuze. The hole is filled with rocks for additional fragmentation.
6 Hand grenade in a can with its arming pin pulled and attached to a tripwire (to pull the grenade out).
7 Hand grenade fastened to a bamboo pole A-frame with a vertical tripwire pegged in the ground.
8 2ft.-long wooden punji stakes hidden in high grass or brush. When ambushed, soldiers on the path would instinctively dive for cover, into these stakes.

Vinh Moc

Vinh Moc Village lies on the coast 19km north of the former DMZ separating North and South Vietnam. In 1965 this region was heavily embattled and declared a "free fire zone." Rather than flee their homes, the villagers went underground, while their thatch huts were leveled by bombing. Many villages prepared underground havens, but Vinh Moc was completely abandoned over 18 months and its inhabitants moved underground for the duration. Four hundred people, 60 families, lived in the labyrinth for six years and life went on with birth, death, and marriage.

The ground consisted of hardened clay. During the rainy season the lower level flooded and puddles of water collected in the upper levels. The tunnels averaged 1m in width and 1.7m in height. The 1,600m of winding tunnels were dug in three levels: 12m, 15m, and 23m. There were reinforced bomb shelters in the two lower levels and families resided in small rooms along these tunnels. There were a communal kitchen, three water wells, an 80-person meeting hall where films were shown, a medical post, a maternity room (where 17 children were born), a school room, lookout posts, a latrine, and a washroom. Of the 13 entrances, seven led on to the beach and the others were scattered among inland hills over a 2 square km area.

The local Militia contingent called the site Outpost 140. The first U-shaped tunnel dug served as a bomb shelter. It was expanded to house the entire village as well as the Militia and military supplies sent from the north. The post served as a supply transfer point to nearby Con Co Island, a departure point for boats infiltrating south, and hundreds of tons of rice were stored there. The tunnel's architect and lead builder, Le Xuan Vy, stated, "It would be meaningless if we could not protect our people. Without the people our post would cease to exist." The complex, while slightly more roomy and developed than most systems, provides an idea of what tunnel systems were like. The Vinh Moc tunnels have been mostly restored and are open to tourists.

Booby traps

Contrary to popular conception, the endless jungles, swamps, paddies, and mountains of Vietnam were not littered with booby traps. Regardless, 11 percent of US dead and 17 percent of the wounded were caused by booby traps. Booby traps were placed around Free World bases and on their patrol routes. They were also placed on routes into and the areas immediately around base camps and those witnessing other VC/NVA activities. The types of booby traps were endless, varying from the crude and simple to the very sophisticated, and employed in endlessly imaginative manners.

Punji stakes were extremely easy to produce and install. Often they were made by civilians as a form of "war tax." Villagers would produce bundles of punji stakes, leaving them at a designated spot outside the village for collection by the VC. These stakes were used for all sorts of traps and obstacles. Hand grenades were widely used in booby traps, mainly being tripwire activated. Other explosive booby traps employed recovered Free World dud mortar and artillery shells, bombs, and just about any other form of munition. Tripwire–activated devices were the most common, but pressure- and command-detonated booby traps were also used along with conventional mines, both anti-personnel and anti-vehicular.

A bamboo punji stake pit. This example was used to orient newly assigned Free World soldiers and is protected by steel grating. (Leroy "Red" Wilson)

An assessment of the fortifications

Overall, the field fortifications employed by the VC/NVA proved to be effective. They were difficult, sometimes virtually impossible, to detect from the ground and air. The VC/NVA's camouflage efforts and ability to blend fortifications into surrounding terrain were excellent. It was not simply the camouflage of individual bunkers and positions, but effective camouflage of large base camps, caches, and other facilities, and they made maximum and effective use of locally available materials. The designs of the fortifications allowed for minimal work, tools, and materials. The average VC/NVA fighter demonstrated at least a basic understanding of simple engineering and fieldcraft skills. The fortifications were also adapted to the local terrain and weather conditions. As simple as the fortifications were, they proved to be extremely resistant to massive Free World firepower. It required a direct hit in most cases to destroy a bunker. While the advanced technology employed by Free World forces (such as "Red Haze" and people-sniffers) aided in locating the elusive enemy, it only went so far. It still required men on the ground "doing it the hard way."

The tunnels, though, were the epitome of the camouflage of the VC/NVA fortification system. By burrowing underground they could sometimes elude Free World forces, and could certainly make it extremely difficult for them to locate and engage the VC/NVA. Even when a tunnel system was discovered, it was enormously difficult to explore the extent, engage the occupants, remove the contents, and neutralize it. The tunnels may not have played a decisive role, but they contributed to the enemy's resilience and perseverance in a long and brutal war. To this day the tunnels of Cu Chi serve as a subterranean monument to the resistance.

The sites today

VC/NVA field fortifications, base camps, and tunnels were temporary in nature and built from non-durable materials. They could last for years but only if properly maintained and not destroyed by flooding. Wood had to be replaced frequently. When the war ended in 1975, most deteriorated within a few years, and little remains today. Traces may occasionally be found, but most of these temporary structures collapsed, were eroded away, were filled in with mud and silt, or were covered by the ever-encroaching jungle. Many densely vegetated areas used as base areas during the war have since been cleared and cultivated. One source claims that 6,250 square miles of the RVN still cannot be used for farming over 30 years after the end of the war. Some of these areas received repeated applications of defoliating chemicals, which killed the roots of trees and brush. This caused erosion, mudslides, and flooding.

However, parts of the formerly extensive Cu Chi and the entire, though smaller, Vinh Moc tunnel complexes have been restored and are open to tourists, complete with tour guides. Cu Chi is 45 miles northwest of Ho Chi Minh City (which even the locals still call Saigon). It has become a major tourist attraction. Cu Chi can be reached by bus from Saigon and the tour fee is only US $4. Tourists can even rent replica VC uniforms, pith helmets, and dummy weapons for use during the tour in order to "fully undergo the VC experience." For US $1 tourists can fire an AK-47. While there are electric lights in most tunnels, flashlights are provided. The tunnels open to tourists have been heightened by 6in. to accommodate Western tourists. It is still a fatiguing trip and not for the claustrophobic. In Saigon itself can be found the Museum of War Remnants with displays of captured weapons and its catalog of horrors. Because of the normalization of relationships between Vietnam and the US, as well as the need to attract tourists, the museum's name was changed from the Museum of American War Crimes. Vinh Moc can be reached by bus from Hue. There are also other war-related sites to visit in the DMZ area.

Vietnam is open to American tourists, but other than memorials to the communist victory and a very few sites like the Cu Chi and Vinh Moc tunnels, there is little to see of the war. American bases have ceased to exist and virtually no signs that they ever existed can be found.